PRESSURE
COOKING

Lakeland and Bauer Media Ltd hereby exclude all liability to the extent permitted by law for any errors or omission in this book and for any loss, damage or expense (whether direct or indirect) suffered by a third party relying on any information contained in this book.

This book was created in 2013 for Lakeland by AWW Books, an imprint of Octopus Publishing Group Ltd, based on materials licensed to it by Bauer Media Books, Sydney.

Bauer Media Limited
54 Park St, Sydney
GPO Box 4088, Sydney, NSW 2001
www.awwcookbooks.com.au

OCTOPUS PUBLISHING GROUP
Design – Chris Bell
Food Director – Pamela Clark

Published for Lakeland in the United Kingdom by Octopus Publishing Group Limited

Endeavour House
189 Shaftesbury Avenue
London WC2H 8JY
United Kingdom
phone + 44 (0) 207 632 5400;
fax + 44 (0) 207 632 5405
aww@octopusbooks.co.uk;
www.octopusbooks.co.uk
www.australian-womens-weekly.com

Printed and bound in China

A catalogue record for this book is available from the British Library.

ISBN 978-1-909770-03-4

The Department of Health advises that eggs should not be consumed raw. This book contains some dishes made with raw or lightly cooked eggs. It is prudent for vulnerable people such as pregnant and nursing mothers, invalids, the elderly, babies and young children to avoid uncooked or lightly cooked dishes made with eggs. Once prepared, these dishes should be kept refrigerated and used promptly.

This book also includes dishes made with nuts and nut derivatives. It is advisable for those with known allergic reactions to nuts and nut derivatives and those who may be potentially vulnerable to these allergies, such as pregnant and nursing mothers, invalids, the elderly, babies and children to avoid dishes made with nuts and nut oils. It is also prudent to check the labels of pre-prepared ingredients for the possible inclusion of nut derivatives.

Some of the recipes in this book have appeared in other publications.

PRESSURE
COOKING

Much loved by previous generations of cooks, pressure cookers are once again firm favourites in the modern kitchen. With this collection of 51 recipes you can prepare delicious soups, stews, curries, roasts and puddings in a fraction of the usual time.

One of an exciting new series of cookbooks from Lakeland, *Pressure Cooking* is packed with delicious colour photos and expert hints, tips and techniques for beginners and experienced cooks alike.

With every recipe triple-tested® for perfect results, these excellent cookbooks are sure to be some of the best-loved on your kitchen bookshelf. To discover the rest of the range, together with our unrivalled selection of creative kitchenware, visit one of our friendly Lakeland stores or shop online at www.lakeland.co.uk.

CONTENTS

ABOUT PRESSURE COOKING

Fast and versatile, pressure cookers are making a comeback in modern kitchens and it's not hard to see why they are becoming so popular.

WHY CHOOSE A PRESSURE COOKER?

The pressure cooker is the perfect appliance for anyone with a busy lifestyle, producing traditionally slow-cooked meals – such as casseroles, soups and curries – significantly faster. Modern pressure cookers can reduce cooking time by up to 60 per cent.

The faster cooking time means that pressure cooking is also economical, saving energy and money. Another bonus is that pressure-cooked food is healthier as the shorter cooking time means more vitamins and minerals are preserved.

Pressure cooked food is full of concentrated flavours because the steam released when ingredients reach a very high temperature is sealed within the cooker, resulting in tender, delicious food. This makes the pressure cooker particularly suitable for the cheaper cuts of meat, which also saves you money. And pulses of all types – dried beans, peas and lentils – tenderise quickly in a pressure cooker, even without soaking.

TYPES OF PRESSURE COOKERS

There are two types of pressure cooker: one you use on the hob and the other is an electric version that is used on the kitchen counter. The size that you choose will depend on your needs; if you have a large family or like to cook in bulk, then a bigger model is the best choice for you.

Hob-top pressure cookers made from aluminium or stainless steel are suitable for either gas or electric hobs but you will need a stainless steel model if you have with a ceramic or induction hob.

SAFE AND EASY TO USE

The pressure cookers of today, both those used on a hob and electric countertop versions, are completely safe and easy to use; their pressure regulators are much more refined than those of pressure cookers used by previous generations.

Always read the instruction manual carefully before you start as, like most appliances, different models have slightly different features.

THE QUICK RELEASE METHOD

For the quick release method referred to in our recipes, use tongs (steam can burn your fingers) to turn the pressure valve on top of the cooker to open the valve and release the steam. This will release the pressure quickly, before you remove the lid. To check the food towards the end of the cooking time or to add more ingredients, follow the quick release method.

NOTE

The recipes in this book use a 5.5-litre pressure cooker. If you have a 3-litre cooker, simply halve the quantities for each recipe.

DO

- Read the instruction manual thoroughly before you use your pressure cooker for the first time
- Read cooking times carefully and begin to time the food after the pressure is reached
- Fill the cooker no further than up to the line marked inside
- Release the lid carefully in an open space and facing away from you to avoid escaping steam
- Use a trivet for steamed puddings and so on
- Use oven gloves if your cooker has metal handles
- Take care when using your cooker when there are children about
- Wash and dry the cooker and removable gasket well after use
- Use a simmer mat to keep the heat as low as possible after your cooker has reached pressure
- Use tongs – not your fingers – to release the pressure from the cooker
- Store the cooker with the lid upside-down

DON'T

- Leave the cooker on and unattended
- Leave an empty cooker on a hot hob
- Overfill the cooker with solid or liquid ingredients
- Cook pasta or porridge or any food that becomes foamy in a pressure cooker
- Soak the bases of the pressure cooker
- Wash the lid of a pressure cooker in a dishwasher as this will damage the valve

COOKING TIMES CHART

FRESH VEGETABLES

Wash and peel vegetables as if you were cooking them by any of the traditional methods. Vegetables cook very fast in a pressure cooker; they're usually cooked on the highest pressure. The times given in the chart on page 9 are only a guide; the cooking time depends on the age of the vegetable, how it has been stored, the size and how the vegetable is chopped. There is a slight difference in cooking times between steaming vegetables over the water in the cooker and cooking them in the water in the cooker; whichever method you choose, it's always better to undercook vegetables; it's easy to add a little more cooking time at the end. Once vegetables are ready, the cooking needs to be stopped immediately. This is done by releasing the pressure on the cooker; check the manual for instructions relating to your own cooker. Frozen vegetables need a little longer than the times suggested in the chart on page 9, but only half a minute or so.

MEAT & CHICKEN

Meat and chicken are usually cooked on the highest pressure and are definitely better in flavour and colour if the meat is browned before pressure cooking. The chart on page 9 is only a guide, as the time taken for meat to cook depends on many factors, such as the age and tenderness of the cut, the temperature of the meat before it goes into the cooker and the size, thickness and weight of the piece or pieces of meat. Be guided for pressure cooking times by individual recipes when cooking large solid pieces of meat – with or without bone. Don't waste money on expensive cuts of meat for the pressure cooker, as they will dry out and be bland in flavour; use the cheaper secondary cuts for the best results. Chicken is easily overcooked in the pressure cooker, especially the boneless fillets.

RICE & OTHER GRAINS

Rice and other grains can be successfully cooked in a pressure cooker. As a guide, you need triple the water to the grain – that is, allow 3 cups water to each 1 cup of grains. Drain away the excess water quickly after the grains are cooked.

Grains such as barley and brown rice are cooked using high pressure, followed by a slow release of pressure – which really means the grains are being cooked more during this release time – followed by a quick release of pressure, this is to stop the cooking. Short rice, such as arborio, is usually cooked using high pressure, then the quick release of pressure to stop the rice overcooking. White rice, including medium and long grain, basmati and jasmine, is cooked using high pressure, then a slow release of pressure, followed by a quick release of pressure.

All grains need a little butter or oil to stop them foaming during the pressure cooking process; about 1 tablespoon of either, for each cup of grain.

All grains along with the water should only half-fill the pressure cooker. Remember rice and most grains go very close to tripling in bulk by the time they're cooked. Season grains with salt before cooking if you like.

The chart on page 9 is a guide only to cooking times for grains; follow the methods in individual recipes. These times are the total cooking times, including the initial time under high pressure and the slow and/or quick release of pressure times.

PULSES

Pulses include all dried beans, peas and lentils. Lentils don't need soaking at all, just washing and draining well like all the other pulses before cooking. Soaking pulses before pressure cooking will reduce the cooking time by 5 to 10 minutes depending on the variety of pulse. Remember that all pulses are dried, so they're going to expand during cooking. Keep this in mind when you're deciding on the quantity to cook; don't over-fill the pressure cooker.

As a guide, only one-third fill the pressure cooker with pulses and water. Don't add salt to the pulses, the salt prevents them from becoming tender. Add 1 teaspoon of butter or vegetable oil for every half cup of pulses; the butter or oil will prevent the mixture from foaming during the cooking time. Pulses are cooked using the highest pressure, and are usually allowed to stand until the pressure releases naturally from the cooker. Always check the manual of your own cooker.

The chart below is only a guide to cooking times; the age and the moisture content of the pulses will determine just how tender the pulses will be after cooking. Pulses appear to store for long periods of time, but in fact are drying out. It's best to buy small quantities often, store them in the fridge, or even better, soak them overnight, drain, and freeze them in portion sizes ready to pressure cook. The cooking times in the chart below are for pulses which have NOT been soaked overnight.

FRESH VEGETABLES

	MINUTES
artichokes (globe) whole	15
asparagus	2
aubergine	2
beans (green)	6
beetroot	20
broad beans	5
broccoli	2
brussels sprouts	7
cabbage	4
carrot	4
cauliflower	2
corn	1
courgette	1
fennel	13
leek	2
okra	10
parsnip	2
peas	2
potato (quarters)	10
pumpkin	8
turnip	5

MEAT & CHICKEN

	MINUTES
beef (chopped coarsely)	10
chicken (whole 1.5 kg)	20
chicken pieces (with bone)	10
chicken fillets (without bone)	5
lamb shanks	25
lamb (chopped coarsely)	20
pork (chopped coarsely)	10
pork ribs (short)	20
veal (chopped coarsely)	10

RICE & OTHER GRAINS

	MINUTES
arborio rice	6
barley	20
brown rice	20
white rice	10

PULSES

	MINUTES
black beans	30
borlotti beans	30
butter beans	40
chickpeas	45
lentils	8
red kidney beans	30
soya beans	35
split peas	20
white beans	30

SOUPS

SPICY CHICKPEA & LENTIL SOUP

200g dried chickpeas
2 teaspoons olive oil
1 medium brown onion (150g),
   chopped finely
3 cloves garlic, crushed
4cm piece fresh ginger (20g),
   grated
2 teaspoons smoked paprika
1 teaspoon each ground cumin
   and coriander
½ teaspoon dried chilli flakes
410g canned tomatoes, crushed
750ml water
750ml chicken stock
2 celery stalks (300g), trimmed,
   sliced thickly
470g pumpkin, cut into 1cm
   pieces
200g red lentils, rinsed, drained
2 tablespoons lime juice
6 tablespoons coarsely chopped
   fresh coriander

1 Place chickpeas in medium bowl, cover with cold water; stand overnight. Rinse under cold water; drain.
2 Heat oil in 5.5-litre pressure cooker; cook onion, garlic and ginger, stirring, until onion softens. Add spices; cook, stirring, until fragrant. Add undrained tomatoes, the water, stock and chickpeas; secure lid. Bring cooker to high pressure. Reduce heat to stabilise pressure; cook 25 minutes.
3 Release pressure using the quick release method (page 6); remove lid. Add celery, pumpkin and lentils; secure lid. Bring cooker to high pressure. Reduce heat to stabilise pressure; cook 5 minutes.
4 Release pressure using the quick release method (page 6); remove lid. Stir in juice and coriander; season to taste.

prep + cook time 40 minutes + standing time
makes 2.5 litres
nutritional count per 250ml 2.4g total fat (0.4g saturated fat); 568kJ (136 cal); 17.2g carbohydrate; 8.5g protein; 6.1g fibre
tips If you have an electric pressure cooker you won't need to reduce the heat to stabilise pressure, your cooker will automatically stabilise itself. Always check with the manufacturer's instructions before using. Recipe suitable to freeze.

CHICKEN & RICE SOUP

2 teaspoons olive oil
1 large brown onion (200g),
 chopped finely
65g white long-grain rice
1 large tomato (220g), chopped
 finely
1 tablespoon drained, finely
 chopped pickled jalapeño
 chillies
good handful coarsely chopped
 fresh coriander
1 large avocado (320g), chopped
 finely

chicken stock
½ chicken (800g)
1 medium carrot (120g), halved
1 small brown onion (80g), halved
1 stalk celery (150g), halved
1 teaspoon black peppercorns
1.5 litres water

1 Make chicken stock. Discard skin and bones from chicken; shred meat coarsely.
2 Heat oil in 5.5-litre pressure cooker; cook onion, stirring, until soft. Add rice; stir to coat in onion mixture. Add stock; secure lid. Bring cooker to high pressure. Reduce heat to stabilise pressure; cook 5 minutes.
3 Release pressure using the quick release method (page 6); remove lid. Return chicken to cooker with tomato and chilli; simmer, uncovered, until hot. Stir in coriander; season to taste. Serve soup topped with avocado.

chicken stock Combine ingredients in 5.5-litre pressure cooker; secure lid. Bring cooker to high pressure. Reduce heat to stabilise pressure; cook 15 minutes. Release pressure using the quick release method (page 6); remove lid. Strain stock into large heatproof bowl. Reserve chicken; discard vegetables and pepper.

prep + cook time 30 minutes
makes 2.75 litres
nutritional count per 250ml
11.4g total fat (2.9g saturated fat); 698kJ (167 cal); 6.9g carbohydrate; 8.7g protein; 1.5g fibre

tips If you have an electric pressure cooker you won't need to reduce the heat to stabilise pressure, your cooker will automatically stabilise itself. Always check with the manufacturer's instructions before using. If making chicken stock for another recipe where you only need the stock, use chicken necks, wings and backs instead of the half chicken. The stock will keep refrigerated for up to 1 week, or frozen for up to 2 months.

GARLIC BEETROOT SOUP

1 tablespoon olive oil

1 medium leek (350g), sliced thinly

4 cloves garlic, crushed

2 tablespoons red wine vinegar

2kg beetroot, peeled, chopped coarsely

1 medium potato (200g), chopped coarsely

1.5 litres water

125ml single cream

1 teaspoon ground cumin

2 teaspoons caraway seeds

1 Heat oil in 5.5-litre pressure cooker; cook leek and garlic, stirring, until leek softens. Add vinegar, beetroot, potato and the water; secure lid. Bring cooker to high pressure. Reduce heat to stabilise pressure; cook 20 minutes. Release pressure using the quick release method (page 6); remove lid. Cool soup mixture 15 minutes.

2 Blend or process soup, in batches, until smooth. Return soup to same cleaned cooker; simmer, uncovered, until hot. Season to taste.

3 Meanwhile, combine cream and cumin in small jug.

4 Serve bowls of soup drizzled with cream; sprinkle with seeds.

prep + cook time 45 minutes
makes 2.25 litres
nutritional count per 250ml
8.4g total fat (4.3g saturated fat); 794kJ (190 cal); 20.2g carbohydrate; 5g protein; 7.3g fibre
tips If you have an electric pressure cooker you won't need to reduce the heat to stabilise pressure, your cooker will automatically stabilise itself. Always check with the manufacturer's instructions before using. Recipe suitable to freeze at the end of step 2.

SCOTCH BROTH

1 tablespoon olive oil
1kg lamb neck chops
100g pearl barley
1 large brown onion (200g),
 chopped coarsely
2 stalks celery (300g), trimmed,
 chopped coarsely
1 large carrot (180g), sliced
 thickly
1.5 litres water
240g finely shredded savoy
 cabbage
handful coarsely chopped fresh
 flat-leaf parsley

1 Heat oil in 5.5-litre pressure cooker; cook lamb, in batches, until browned. Remove from cooker.
2 Return lamb to cooker with barley, onion, celery, carrot and the water; secure lid. Bring cooker to high pressure. Reduce heat to stabilise pressure; cook 20 minutes.
3 Release pressure using the quick release method (page 6); remove lid. Remove lamb with slotted spoon. Add cabbage to cooker; secure lid. Bring cooker to high pressure. Reduce heat to stabilise pressure; cook 5 minutes.
4 Meanwhile, remove meat from lamb chops; discard bones, chop meat coarsely.
5 Release pressure using the quick release method (page 6); remove lid. Stir in lamb and parsley; season to taste.

prep + cook time 40 minutes
makes 3 litres
nutritional count per 250ml
9.5g total fat (3.7g saturated fat); 727kJ (174 cal); 7.4g carbohydrate; 13.6g protein; 2.8g fibre
tips If you have an electric pressure cooker you won't need to reduce the heat to stabilise pressure, your cooker will automatically stabilise itself. Always check with the manufacturer's instructions before using. Recipe suitable to freeze.

WHITE BEAN & CHORIZO SOUP

300g dried white beans
1.5 litres water
60ml olive oil
4 cloves garlic, crushed
4 tablespoons coarsely chopped
   fresh flat-leaf parsley
170g cured chorizo, halved
   lengthways, thinly sliced

1 Place beans in medium bowl, cover with cold water; stand overnight. Rinse under cold water; drain.
2 Combine beans and the water in 5.5-litre pressure cooker; secure lid. Bring cooker to high pressure. Reduce heat to stabilise pressure; cook 20 minutes. Release pressure using the quick release method (page 6); remove lid. Drain beans; reserve 750ml cooking liquid. Blend beans and reserved cooking liquid in batches until smooth.
3 Heat 2 tablespoons of the oil in cooker; stir in garlic, half the parsley and puréed beans. Simmer, uncovered, 5 minutes. Season to taste.
4 Meanwhile, heat remaining oil in large frying pan; cook chorizo until browned and crisp.
5 Top soup with remaining parsley and chorizo and drizzle with chorizo cooking oil before serving.
6 Serve with toasted bread, if liked.

prep + cook time 35 minutes + standing time
makes 1.75 litres
nutritional count per 250ml 16.1g total fat (3.9g saturated fat); 1170kJ (280 cal); 15.7g carbohydrate; 14.3g protein; 8.5g fibre
tips If you have an electric pressure cooker you won't need to reduce the heat to stabilise pressure, your cooker will automatically stabilise itself. Always check the manufacturer's instructions before using. You can use dried cannellini, haricot or butter beans for this recipe. Recipe not suitable to freeze.

MEDITERRANEAN VEGETABLE SOUP

1 tablespoon olive oil
200g chestnut mushrooms,
    quartered
1 large red onion (300g), chopped
    coarsely
3 cloves garlic, crushed
handful coarsely chopped fresh
    basil
1 medium aubergine (300g),
    chopped coarsely
2 medium red peppers (400g),
    chopped coarsely
1 large courgette (150g),
    chopped coarsely
800g canned tomatoes, crushed
500ml water

1 Heat half the oil in 5.5-litre pressure cooker; cook mushrooms until browned lightly. Remove from cooker.

2 Heat remaining oil in cooker; cook onion, garlic and half the basil, stirring, until onion softens. Add aubergine, pepper, courgette, undrained tomatoes and the water; secure lid. Bring cooker to high pressure. Reduce heat to stabilise pressure; cook 5 minutes.

3 Release pressure using the quick release method (page 6); remove lid. Add mushrooms; simmer, uncovered, until hot. Season to taste. Serve soup sprinkled with remaining basil.

prep + cook time 20 minutes
makes 2.5 litres
nutritional count per 250ml
2.3g total fat (0.3g saturated fat); 276kJ (66 cal); 6.7g carbohydrate; 2.9g protein; 3.4g fibre
tips If you have an electric pressure cooker you won't need to reduce the heat to stabilise pressure, your cooker will automatically stabilise itself. Always check with the manufacturer's instructions before using. Recipe not suitable to freeze.

CHICKEN CONGEE

1 tablespoon groundnut oil
200g jasmine rice
4cm piece fresh ginger (20g), grated
1 spring onion, sliced thinly
1 fresh long red chilli, sliced thinly
1 tablespoon light soy sauce

chicken stock
½ chicken (800g)
1 medium carrot (120g), halved
1 small brown onion (80g), halved
1 stalk celery (150g), trimmed, halved
1 teaspoon black peppercorns
2 litres water

1 Make chicken stock. Discard skin and bones from chicken; shred meat coarsely.
2 Heat oil in 5.5-litre pressure cooker; cook rice, stirring, 2 minutes. Add stock and ginger; secure lid. Bring cooker to high pressure. Reduce heat to stabilise pressure; cook 10 minutes.
3 Release pressure using the quick release method (page 6); remove lid. Stir chicken into cooker, reheat. Serve soup topped with onion, chilli and sauce.

chicken stock Combine ingredients in 5.5-litre pressure cooker; secure lid. Bring cooker to high pressure. Reduce heat to stabilise pressure; cook 15 minutes. Release pressure using the quick release method (page 6); remove lid. Strain stock into large heatproof bowl. Reserve chicken; discard vegetables and pepper.

prep + cook time 40 minutes
makes 2 litres
nutritional count per 250ml
10.5g total fat (2.9g saturated fat); 966kJ (231 cal); 21.5g carbohydrate; 12g protein; 1g fibre
tips If you have an electric pressure cooker you won't need to reduce the heat to stabilise pressure, your cooker will automatically stabilise itself. Always check with the manufacturer's instructions before using. If making chicken stock for another recipe where you only need the stock, use chicken necks, wings and backs instead. The stock will keep refrigerated for up to 1 week, or frozen for up to 2 months. Congee not suitable to freeze.

LAMB SHANK, VEGETABLE & LENTIL SOUP

2 tablespoons olive oil
3 french-trimmed lamb shanks
(750g)
1 medium brown onion (150g),
chopped finely
2 cloves garlic, crushed
2 medium carrots (240g),
chopped coarsely
2 celery stalks (300g), trimmed,
chopped coarsely
155g piece of pancetta, chopped
coarsely
1.25 litres water
125ml dry white wine
130g puy lentils, rinsed, drained
60g frozen peas

1 Heat half the oil in 5.5-litre pressure cooker; cook lamb, in batches, until browned. Remove from cooker.

2 Heat remaining oil in cooker; cook onion, garlic, carrot, celery and pancetta, stirring, until vegetables soften. Return lamb to cooker with the water and wine; secure lid. Bring cooker to high pressure. Reduce heat to stabilise pressure; cook 20 minutes.

3 Release pressure using the quick release method (page 6); remove lid. Add lentils; secure lid. Bring cooker to high pressure. Reduce heat to stabilise pressure; cook 10 minutes.

4 Release pressure using the quick release method (page 6); remove lid. Remove lamb; when cool enough to handle shred meat coarsely, discard bones. Return lamb to cooker with peas; simmer, uncovered until peas are tender. Season to taste.

prep + cook time 40 minutes
makes 2 litres
nutritional count per 250ml
10.5g total fat (3g saturated fat); 957kJ (229 cal); 9.5g carbohydrate; 19.6g protein; 4.2g fibre
tips If you have an electric pressure cooker you won't need to reduce the heat to stabilise pressure, your cooker will automatically stabilise itself. Always check with the manufacturer's instructions before using. Recipe suitable to freeze.

HEARTY BEEF & VEGETABLE SOUP

2 tablespoons olive oil
750g braising steak, chopped
  coarsely
1 large brown onion (200g),
  chopped coarsely
2 cloves garlic, crushed
1 litre water
410g canned tomatoes, crushed
1 celery stalk (150g), trimmed,
  chopped coarsely
1 medium carrot (120g), chopped
  coarsely
½ small cauliflower (500g), cut
  into florets
1 large courgette (150g),
  chopped coarsely
60g frozen peas
60g frozen corn

1 Heat half the oil in 5.5-litre
pressure cooker; cook beef, in
batches, until browned. Remove
from cooker.
2 Heat remaining oil in cooker;
cook onion and garlic, stirring,
until onion softens. Return beef
to cooker with the water and
undrained tomatoes; secure lid.
Bring cooker to high pressure.
Reduce heat to stabilise pressure;
cook 25 minutes.
3 Release pressure using the
quick release method (page 6);
remove lid. Add celery, carrot,
cauliflower and courgette; secure
lid. Bring cooker to high pressure.
Reduce heat to stabilise pressure;
cook 3 minutes.
4 Release pressure using the
quick release method (page 6);
remove lid. Add peas and corn;
simmer, uncovered until peas are
tender. Season to taste.

prep + cook time 40 minutes
makes 3 litres
nutritional count per 250ml
6.2g total fat (1.6g saturated fat);
581kJ (139 cal); 4.8g carbohydrate;
14.8g protein; 2.6g fibre
tips If you have an electric
pressure cooker you won't need
to reduce the heat to stabilise
pressure, your cooker will
automatically stabilise itself. Always
check with the manufacturer's
instructions before using. Recipe
suitable to freeze.

PEA, HAM & BROAD BEAN SOUP

1 tablespoon olive oil
1 large brown onion (200g),
    chopped coarsely
2 cloves garlic, crushed
2 celery stalks (300g), trimmed,
    chopped coarsely
1 medium carrot (120g), chopped
    coarsely
1 ham hock (750g)
2 dried bay leaves
2 litres water
225g frozen broad beans, peeled
300g green split peas, rinsed,
    drained

mint sauce
2 good handfuls fresh mint leaves
60ml olive oil
2 tablespoons white wine vinegar
2 teaspoons caster sugar

1 Heat oil in 5.5-litre pressure
cooker; cook onion, garlic, celery
and carrot, stirring, about
3 minutes or until vegetables
soften. Add ham, bay leaves and
the water; secure lid. Bring
cooker to high pressure. Reduce
heat to stabilise pressure; cook
20 minutes.
2 Release pressure using the
quick release method (page 6);
remove lid. Add beans and peas;
secure lid. Bring cooker to high
pressure. Reduce heat to stabilise
pressure; cook 20 minutes.
3 Release pressure using the
quick release method (page 6);
remove lid. Discard bay leaves.
Remove ham. Cool soup
10 minutes.
4 Meanwhile, discard skin, fat
and bone from ham; shred meat
coarsely.
5 Blend or process soup, in
batches, until smooth. Return
soup to cooker; stir in ham.
Simmer, uncovered, until hot;
season to taste.
6 Meanwhile, make mint sauce.
7 Serve bowls of soup drizzled
with mint sauce.

mint sauce Blend ingredients
until smooth.

prep + cook time 1 hour
10 minutes
makes 1.5 litres
nutritional count per 250ml
18.3g total fat (3.5g saturated fat);
1751kJ (419 cal); 32g carbohydrate;
26.1g protein; 11.1g fibre
tips If you have an electric
pressure cooker you won't need
to reduce the heat to stabilise
pressure, your cooker will
automatically stabilise itself. Always
check with the manufacturer's
instructions before using. Soup
suitable to freeze; mint sauce not
suitable to freeze.

CHICKEN

COQ AU VIN

12 baby brown onions (300g)
2 tablespoons olive oil
3 rindless bacon rashers (195g),
  chopped coarsely
315g button mushrooms
3 cloves garlic, crushed
2 tablespoons plain flour
4 chicken thighs (800g)
4 chicken drumsticks (600g)
70g tomato paste
250ml dry red wine
2 dried bay leaves
6 sprigs fresh thyme

1 Peel onions, leaving root ends intact. Heat 2 teaspoons of the oil in 5.5-litre pressure cooker; cook onions, stirring, until browned lightly. Remove from cooker.
2 Heat another 2 teaspoons of the oil in cooker; cook bacon, mushrooms and garlic, stirring, until browned lightly. Remove from cooker.
3 Season flour in large bowl; add chicken, toss to coat in flour. Shake off excess. Heat remaining oil in cooker; cook chicken, in batches, until browned. Remove from cooker.
4 Return chicken to cooker with onions, bacon mixture, paste, wine, bay leaves and thyme; secure lid. Bring cooker to high pressure. Reduce heat to stabilise pressure; cook 10 minutes.
5 Release pressure using the quick release method (page 6); remove lid. Season to taste; serve sprinkled with thyme leaves and accompanied by creamy mashed potato, if liked.

prep + cook time 30 minutes
serves 4
nutritional count per serving
47.7g total fat (13.9g saturated fat); 3035kJ (726 cal); 10g carbohydrate; 53.5g protein; 2.2g fibre
tips If you have an electric pressure cooker you won't need to reduce the heat to stabilise pressure, your cooker will automatically stabilise itself. Always check with the manufacturer's instructions before using. Recipe not suitable to freeze.

BUTTER CHICKEN

4 chicken leg portions (1.4kg)
1 tablespoon lemon juice
140g natural yogurt
5cm piece fresh ginger (25g),
    grated
2 teaspoons garam masala
1 tablespoon vegetable oil
40g butter
1 medium brown onion (150g),
    chopped finely
4 cloves garlic, crushed
1 teaspoon each ground
    coriander, cumin, cinnamon
    and hot paprika
2 tablespoons tomato paste
410g tomato passata
125ml chicken stock
2 tablespoons honey
80ml single cream
6 tablespoons fresh coriander
    leaves

1 Combine chicken, juice, yogurt, ginger and garam masala in large bowl. Heat half the oil and half the butter in 5.5-litre pressure cooker; cook chicken, in batches, until browned. Remove from cooker.

2 Heat remaining oil and butter in cooker; cook onion and garlic, stirring, until onion softens. Add spices; cook, stirring, until fragrant. Return chicken to cooker with paste, passata, stock and honey; secure lid. Bring cooker to high pressure. Reduce heat to stabilise pressure; cook 20 minutes.

3 Release pressure using the quick release method (page 6); remove lid. Stir in cream; season to taste. Serve chicken sprinkled with coriander and accompanied by steamed basmati rice, if liked.

prep + cook time 40 minutes
serves 4
nutritional count per serving
58.1g total fat (23.5g saturated fat); 3403kJ (814 cal); 23.5g carbohydrate; 48.7g protein; 4g fibre

tips If you have an electric pressure cooker you won't need to reduce the heat to stabilise pressure, your cooker will automatically stabilise itself. Always check with the manufacturer's instructions before using. Recipe not suitable to freeze.

CHICKEN & FIG TAGINE

2 tablespoons plain flour
4 chicken breasts on the bone
(1kg)
2 tablespoons olive oil
1 large red onion (300g), sliced
thinly
2 cloves garlic, crushed
2 teaspoons each ground cumin,
coriander, ginger and cinnamon
pinch saffron threads
180ml chicken stock
1 tablespoon honey
315g spinach, trimmed, shredded
coarsely
6 medium fresh figs (360g),
halved
1 teaspoon caster sugar
2 tablespoons each coarsely
chopped fresh flat-leaf parsley
and coriander
70g roasted unsalted pistachios,
coarsely chopped

1 Season flour in large bowl; add chicken, toss to coat in flour. Shake off excess. Heat half the oil in 5.5-litre pressure cooker; cook chicken, in batches, until browned. Remove from cooker.

2 Heat remaining oil in cooker; cook onion, garlic and spices, stirring, until onion softens. Return chicken to cooker with stock and honey; secure lid. Bring cooker to high pressure. Reduce heat to stabilise pressure; cook 15 minutes.

3 Release pressure using the quick release method (page 6); remove lid. Remove chicken; cover to keep warm. Stir spinach into cooker; season to taste.

4 Place figs, cut-side up, on baking-parchment-lined oven tray; sprinkle with sugar. Cook under preheated grill about 5 minutes or until figs are browned lightly.

5 Return chicken to cooker; simmer, uncovered, until hot. Serve tagine topped with figs; sprinkle with herbs and nuts.

prep + cook time 30 minutes
serves 4
nutritional count per serving
39g total fat (8.5g saturated fat); 2742kJ (656 cal); 25.9g carbohydrate; 48g protein; 7.5g fibre

tips If you have an electric pressure cooker you won't need to reduce the heat to stabilise pressure, your cooker will automatically stabilise itself. Always check with the manufacturer's instructions before using. Recipe suitable to freeze without figs.

CHICKEN CACCIATORE

2 tablespoons olive oil
4 chicken thighs (800g)
4 chicken drumsticks (600g)
1 medium brown onion (150g),
   sliced thinly
2 cloves garlic, crushed
2 drained anchovy fillets,
   chopped finely
2 tablespoons white wine vinegar
70g tomato paste
125ml dry red wine
410g canned tomatoes, crushed
60g pitted black olives
6 tablespoons coarsely chopped
   fresh flat-leaf parsley

1 Heat half the oil in 5.5-litre pressure cooker; cook chicken, in batches, until browned. Remove from cooker.
2 Heat remaining oil in cooker; cook onion, garlic and anchovies, stirring, until onion softens. Return chicken to cooker with vinegar, paste, wine and undrained tomatoes; secure lid. Bring cooker to high pressure. Reduce heat to stabilise pressure; cook 10 minutes.
3 Release pressure using the quick release method (page 6); remove lid. Stir in olives and parsley; season to taste.
4 Serve with creamy mashed potato or crusty bread, if liked.

prep + cook time 30 minutes
serves 4
nutritional count per serving
41.6g total fat (11.6g saturated fat); 2587kJ (619 cal); 10.6g carbohydrate; 44.6g protein; 3.2g fibre
tips If you have an electric pressure cooker you won't need to reduce the heat to stabilise pressure, your cooker will automatically stabilise itself. Always check with the manufacturer's instructions before using. Recipe suitable to freeze.

GREEN CHICKEN CURRY

1 tablespoon groundnut oil
1kg boneless, skinless chicken
    thighs, quartered
75g green curry paste
250ml coconut cream
2 medium courgettes (240g),
    sliced thickly
1 tablespoon fish sauce
1 tablespoon lime juice
1 tablespoon grated palm sugar
4 tablespoons each fresh
    coriander and thai basil leaves
2 spring onions, sliced thinly

1 Heat half the oil in 5.5-litre pressure cooker; cook chicken, in batches, until browned. Remove from cooker.
2 Heat remaining oil in cooker; cook paste, stirring, about 3 minutes or until fragrant. Return chicken to cooker with coconut cream; secure lid. Bring cooker to high pressure. Reduce heat to stabilise pressure; cook 5 minutes.
3 Release pressure using the quick release method (page 6); remove lid. Add courgettes; secure lid. Bring cooker to high pressure. Reduce heat to stabilise pressure; cook 2 minutes.
4 Release pressure using the quick release method (page 6); remove lid. Stir in sauce, juice, sugar and half the herbs; season to taste. Serve sprinkled with remaining herbs and onion accompanied by steamed jasmine rice, if liked.

prep + cook time 20 minutes
serves 4
nutritional count per serving
41.6g total fat (18.3g saturated fat); 2562kJ (613 cal); 8.6g carbohydrate; 50.1g protein; 4.4g fibre

tips If you have an electric pressure cooker you won't need to reduce the heat to stabilise pressure, your cooker will automatically stabilise itself. Always check with the manufacturer's instructions before using. Recipe not suitable to freeze. If you can't find thai basil, you can substitute a mix of basil and mint leaves.

CHICKEN WITH PEPPERS

1 tablespoon olive oil

4 chicken thighs (800g)

2 medium brown onions (300g),
   sliced thinly

3 cloves garlic, crushed

2 medium red peppers (400g),
   sliced thickly

2 medium yellow peppers (400g),
   sliced thickly

1 tablespoon tomato paste

80ml dry white wine

80ml chicken stock

2 dried bay leaves

4 sprigs fresh thyme

2 teaspoons finely chopped fresh
   thyme

1 Heat half the oil in 5.5-litre pressure cooker; cook chicken, in batches, until browned. Remove from cooker.

2 Heat remaining oil in cooker; cook onion, garlic and peppers, stirring, until onion softens. Add paste; cook, stirring, 1 minute. Return chicken to cooker with wine, stock, bay leaves and thyme sprigs; secure lid. Bring cooker to high pressure. Reduce heat to stabilise pressure; cook 15 minutes.

3 Release pressure using the quick release method (page 6); remove lid. Season to taste. Serve sprinkled with chopped thyme and accompanied by mashed potato, if liked.

prep + cook time 30 minutes
serves 4
nutritional count per serving
25g total fat (7.3g saturated fat); 1634kJ (391 cal); 10.1g carbohydrate; 27g protein; 3g fibre

tips If you have an electric pressure cooker you won't need to reduce the heat to stabilise pressure, your cooker will automatically stabilise itself. Always check with the manufacturer's instructions before using. Recipe suitable to freeze.

MEXICAN KIDNEY BEANS & SAUSAGES

300g dried red kidney beans
1 dried bay leaf
1.5 litres water
1 tablespoon olive oil
4 chicken sausages (480g)
170g cured chorizo, thinly sliced
1 large brown onion (200g),
  chopped finely
4 cloves garlic, crushed
1 tablespoon ground cumin
2 teaspoons ground coriander
280g bottled tomato pasta sauce
1 medium red pepper (200g),
  sliced thinly
2 fresh long green chillies,
  chopped finely
1 medium tomato (150g),
  deseeded, chopped finely
4 tablespoons coarsely chopped
  fresh coriander

1 Place beans in medium bowl, cover with cold water; stand overnight. Rinse under cold water; drain.
2 Combine beans, bay leaf and the water in 5.5-litre pressure cooker; secure lid. Bring cooker to high pressure. Reduce heat to stabilise pressure; cook 15 minutes.
3 Release pressure using the quick release method (page 6); remove lid. Drain beans; reserve 250ml cooking liquid, discard bay leaf.
4 Heat oil in same cleaned cooker; cook sausages until browned. Remove from cooker; slice thickly. Discard oil from cooker; cook chorizo until browned. Add onion and garlic; cook, stirring, until onion softens. Add spices; cook, stirring, until fragrant. Return beans to cooker with sausages, sauce, pepper and reserved cooking liquid; secure lid. Bring cooker to high pressure. Reduce heat to stabilise pressure; cook 8 minutes.
5 Release pressure using the quick release method (page 6); remove lid. Season to taste. Serve sprinkled with combined chilli, tomato and coriander and accompanied by a dollop of soured cream and tortilla chips, if liked.

prep + cook time 40 minutes + standing time
serves 4
nutritional count per serving
46.5g total fat (14.6g saturated fat); 3319kJ (794 cal); 41.9g carbohydrate; 41.9g protein; 22.8g fibre

tips If you have an electric pressure cooker you won't need to reduce the heat to stabilise pressure, your cooker will automatically stabilise itself. Always check with the manufacturer's instructions before using. This is a great option for a easy dinner party with friends. Simply double the quantities to serve 8. You can cook the dish up to step 5 the day before and chop the chillies, tomato and coriander a few hours before serving. This dish also freezes well.

GREEK-STYLE ROAST CHICKEN

1.6kg whole chicken
1 medium lemon (140g), cut into
   wedges
6 cloves garlic, unpeeled
6 sprigs fresh oregano
1 tablespoon olive oil
250ml chicken stock
125ml dry white wine

1 Rinse chicken under cold water; pat dry. Push lemon, garlic and oregano into chicken cavity. Tuck wing tips under; tie legs together with kitchen string. Season.
2 Heat oil in 5.5-litre pressure cooker; cook chicken until browned all over. Remove from cooker. Add stock and wine to cooker; place chicken on oiled wire rack in cooker. Secure lid; bring cooker to high pressure. Reduce heat to stabilise pressure; cook 30 minutes.
3 Release pressure using the quick release method (page 6); remove lid. Remove chicken, cover; stand 10 minutes before serving. Discard cooking liquid or reserve for use as stock.

prep + cook time 45 minutes
serves 6
nutritional count per serving
24.8g total fat (7.2g saturated fat); 1463kJ (350 cal); 1.1g carbohydrate; 27.4g protein; 1.1g fibre

tips If you have an electric pressure cooker you won't need to reduce the heat to stabilise pressure, your cooker will automatically stabilise itself. Always check with the manufacturer's instructions before using. Recipe not suitable to freeze.

PORK

CARAMELISED PEPPER PORK

3 shallots (75g), chopped finely
2 cloves garlic, crushed
2 tablespoons fish sauce
1 tablespoon ground black
  pepper
800g boneless pork belly, rind
  removed, chopped coarsely
1 tablespoon groundnut oil
2 tablespoons dark brown sugar
80ml water
2 spring onions, sliced finely

1 Combine shallot, garlic, sauce, pepper and pork in large bowl.
2 Heat oil in 5.5-litre pressure cooker; cook pork, in batches, until browned. Remove from cooker.
3 Return pork to cooker with sugar; cook, stirring, until sugar caramelises. Add the water; secure lid. Bring cooker to high pressure. Reduce heat to stabilise pressure; cook 20 minutes.
4 Release pressure using the quick release method (page 6); remove lid. Serve sprinkled with onion accompanied by steamed rice, if liked.

prep + cook time 35 minutes
serves 4
nutritional count per serving
43g total fat (13.9g saturated fat); 2270kJ (543 cal); 7.5g carbohydrate; 32.3g protein; 0.6g fibre
tips If you have an electric pressure cooker you won't need to reduce the heat to stabilise pressure, your cooker will automatically stabilise itself. Always check with the manufacturer's instructions before using. Recipe suitable to freeze.

MAPLE SYRUP PORK STEW

1 tablespoon olive oil
1kg pork neck, chopped coarsely
1 medium brown onion (150g),
    chopped finely
2 cloves garlic, crushed
60ml maple syrup
60ml orange juice
125ml chicken stock
280g baby carrots, trimmed
2 celery stalks (300g), trimmed,
    cut into thick matchsticks
2 tablespoons currants
100g baby spinach leaves

1 Heat half the oil in 5.5-litre pressure cooker; cook pork, in batches, until browned. Remove from cooker.

2 Heat remaining oil in cooker; cook onion and garlic, stirring, until onion softens. Return pork to cooker with syrup, juice and stock; secure lid. Bring cooker to high pressure. Reduce heat to stabilise pressure; cook 20 minutes.

3 Release pressure using the quick release method (page 6); remove lid. Add carrots, celery and currants; secure lid. Bring cooker to high pressure. Reduce heat to stabilise pressure; cook 5 minutes.

4 Release pressure using the quick release method (page 6); remove lid. Stir in spinach; season to taste.

prep + cook time 35 minutes
serves 4
nutritional count per serving
25g total fat (7.5g saturated fat); 2328kJ (557 cal); 25g carbohydrate; 55.5g protein; 4.7g fibre
tips If you have an electric pressure cooker you won't need to reduce the heat to stabilise pressure, your cooker will automatically stabilise itself. Always check with the manufacturer's instructions before using. Recipe suitable to freeze.

HAM HOCK WITH LENTILS

1 ham hock (1kg)
1 dried bay leaf
1 litre water
2 tablespoons olive oil
1 large brown onion (200g),
  chopped finely
2 cloves garlic, crushed
2 tablespoons tomato paste
1 medium (120g) carrot, chopped
  coarsely
300g puy lentils
4 tablespoons coarsely chopped
  fresh flat-leaf parsley

1 Combine ham, bay leaf and the water in 5.5-litre pressure cooker; secure lid. Bring cooker to high pressure. Reduce heat to stabilise pressure; cook 15 minutes.

2 Release pressure using the quick release method (page 6); remove lid. Strain mixture over large heatproof bowl. Reserve ham and 750ml cooking liquid; discard bay leaf.

3 Heat oil in cooker; add onion and garlic, cook, stirring, until onion softens. Return ham to cooker with reserved cooking liquid, paste, carrot and lentils; secure lid. Bring cooker to high pressure. Reduce heat to stabilise pressure; cook 15 minutes.

4 Release pressure using the quick release method (page 6); remove lid, season to taste. Remove ham from cooker. When cool enough to handle remove ham from bone, chop ham coarsely; discard skin, fat and bone. Return ham to cooker, reheat before serving. Sprinkle with parsley and serve with a salad of baby spinach, if liked.

prep + cook time 35 minutes
serves 4
nutritional count per serving
21.9g total fat (5.6g saturated fat); 2349kJ (562 cal); 33.8g carbohydrate; 53.3g protein; 12.6g fibre

tips If you have an electric pressure cooker you won't need to reduce the heat to stabilise pressure, your cooker will automatically stabilise itself. Always check with the manufacturer's instructions before using. Recipe not suitable to freeze.

PORK SAUSAGE & FENNEL RISOTTO

6 pork sausages (380g)
1 tablespoon olive oil
20g butter
1 medium brown onion (150g),
  chopped finely
1 medium fennel bulb (300g),
  trimmed, chopped finely
1 clove garlic, crushed
300g arborio rice
125ml dry white wine
875ml chicken stock
500ml water
60g frozen peas
40g finely grated parmesan
  cheese
2 teaspoons finely chopped fresh
  thyme

1 Cook sausages in heated 5.5-litre pressure cooker until browned. Remove from cooker; slice thinly.
2 Heat oil and butter in cooker; cook onion, fennel and garlic, stirring, until vegetables soften. Add rice; stir to coat in butter mixture. Add wine; simmer, uncovered, until liquid is absorbed. Add stock and the water; secure lid. Bring cooker to high pressure. Reduce heat to stabilise pressure; cook 7 minutes.
3 Release pressure using the quick release method (page 6); remove lid. Add sausage and peas; cover, stand 5 minutes. Stir in half the cheese and thyme; season to taste.
4 Serve risotto sprinkled with remaining cheese.

prep + cook time 25 minutes
serves 4
nutritional count per serving
34.4g total fat (14.5g saturated fat); 2964kJ (709 cal); 68.3g carbohydrate; 24.6g protein; 4.5g fibre
tips If you have an electric pressure cooker you won't need to reduce the heat to stabilise pressure, your cooker will automatically stabilise itself. Always check with the manufacturer's instructions before using. Recipe not suitable to freeze.

STICKY PORK SPARE RIBS

1.5kg pork spare ribs
250ml water
115g orange marmalade
80ml kecap manis
4 cloves garlic, crushed
8cm piece fresh ginger (40g), grated
2 teaspoons five-spice powder

1 Combine ribs and the water in 5.5-litre pressure cooker; secure lid. Bring cooker to high pressure. Reduce heat to stabilise pressure; cook 15 minutes.

2 Meanwhile, combine remaining ingredients in large bowl. Preheat grill.

3 Release cooker pressure using the quick release method (page 6); remove lid. Drain ribs; combine with marmalade mixture. Place ribs, in single layer, on oiled wire rack over large shallow baking dish filled with 1cm water. Grill ribs about 8 minutes or until browned, turning halfway through cooking time and brushing occasionally with remaining marmalade mixture.

prep + cook time 20 minutes
serves 4
nutritional count per serving
13.6g total fat (4.6g saturated fat); 1484kJ (355 cal); 20.2g carbohydrate; 37.2g protein; 1g fibre
tips If you have an electric pressure cooker you won't need to reduce the heat to stabilise pressure, your cooker will automatically stabilise itself. Always check with the manufacturer's instructions before using. Recipe not suitable to freeze.

HUNGARIAN PORK CABBAGE ROLLS

410g jar sauerkraut
10 large cabbage leaves (500g)
1 tablespoon olive oil
50g streaky bacon, chopped
   finely
1 large brown onion (200g),
   chopped finely
3 cloves garlic, crushed
300g minced pork
100g long-grain white rice
2 teaspoons smoked paprika
1 teaspoon ground allspice
410g canned tomato purée
250ml water
60g soured cream
2 tablespoons finely chopped
   flat-leaf parsley

1 Drain sauerkraut; place in large bowl. Cover sauerkraut with cold water, stand 15 minutes; drain. Rinse under cold water; drain.
2 Meanwhile, trim large stems from cabbage leaves. Boil, steam or microwave leaves until pliable; drain. Rinse under cold water; drain. Pat dry with absorbent paper.
3 Heat oil in 5.5-litre pressure cooker; cook bacon, onion and garlic, stirring, until onion softens. Remove from cooker; cool.
4 Combine onion mixture, pork, rice and spices in medium bowl; season.
5 Place one cabbage leaf, vein-side up, on board; cut leaf in half lengthways. Place heaped tablespoons of pork mixture at stem end of each piece of cabbage; roll cabbage tightly over filling, fold in sides. Continue rolling to enclose filling. Repeat with remaining cabbage and pork mixture.
6 Place sauerkraut in cooker; top with cabbage rolls, seam-side down. Combine purée and the water; pour over rolls. Secure lid;

bring cooker to high pressure. Reduce heat to stabilise pressure; cook 10 minutes.
7 Release pressure using the quick release method (page 6); remove lid. Remove rolls from cooker. Stir soured cream into sauerkraut mixture; simmer, uncovered, until hot, season to taste. Serve sauerkraut topped with rolls and flat-leaf parsley.

prep + cook time 50 minutes + standing time
makes 12
nutritional count per roll
6.1g total fat (2.4g saturated fat); 577kJ (138 cal); 10.9g carbohydrate; 8.4g protein; 3.5g fibre
tips If you have an electric pressure cooker you won't need to reduce the heat to stabilise pressure, your cooker will automatically stabilise itself. Always check with the manufacturer's instructions before using. Recipe not suitable to freeze.

ITALIAN CHILLI BRAISED PORK

800g boned pork shoulder
2 tablespoons olive oil
4 cloves garlic, crushed
4 drained anchovy fillets,
    chopped finely
410g canned chopped tomatoes
60ml water
2 tablespoons finely chopped
    fresh oregano
1 tablespoon rinsed drained
    capers
½ teaspoon dried chilli flakes
75g pitted kalamata olives

1 Roll pork tightly; tie with kitchen string, at 2cm intervals, to secure. Season pork. Heat half the oil in 5.5-litre pressure cooker; cook pork until browned all over. Remove from cooker.

2 Heat remaining oil in cooker; cook garlic and anchovy, stirring, until fragrant. Stir in undrained tomatoes, the water, oregano, capers and chilli. Return pork to cooker; secure lid. Bring cooker to high pressure. Reduce heat to stabilise pressure; cook 25 minutes.

3 Release pressure using the quick release method (page 6); remove lid. Remove pork, cover; stand 5 minutes then slice thinly. Stir olives into sauce; season to taste. Serve pork with sauce. Sprinkle with some extra oregano and serve with creamy polenta, if you like.

prep + cook time 30 minutes
serves 4
nutritional count per serving
26g total fat (6.8g saturated fat); 1868kJ (447 cal); 8.1g carbohydrate; 44.6g protein; 2g fibre

tips If you have an electric pressure cooker you won't need to reduce the heat to stabilise pressure, your cooker will automatically stabilise itself. Always check with the manufacturer's instructions before using. If cooked slightly pink, pork is very tender and moist. If you prefer it well done, cook it for 2 minutes longer. Recipe not suitable to freeze.

PORK, FENNEL & OLIVE RAGOUT

2 tablespoons plain flour
1kg pork neck, chopped coarsely
1 tablespoon olive oil
1 medium leek (350g), sliced
  thinly
1 medium fennel bulb (300g),
  trimmed, sliced thinly
2 cloves garlic, crushed
80ml dry white wine
125ml chicken stock
2 tablespoons white balsamic
  vinegar
60g pitted mixed olives
2 tablespoons coarsely chopped
  fresh flat-leaf parsley

1 Season flour in large bowl; add pork, toss to coat in flour. Shake off excess. Heat half the oil in 5.5-litre pressure cooker; cook pork, in batches, until browned. Remove from cooker.

2 Heat remaining oil in cooker; cook leek, fennel and garlic, stirring, until vegetables soften. Return pork to cooker with wine, stock and vinegar; secure lid. Bring cooker to high pressure. Reduce heat to stabilise pressure; cook 30 minutes.

3 Release pressure using the quick release method (page 6); remove lid. Stir in olives; season to taste. Serve ragout sprinkled with parsley.

prep + cook time 45 minutes
serves 4
nutritional count per serving
25.2g total fat (7.5g saturated fat); 2149kJ (514 cal); 11.2g carbohydrate; 55.7g protein; 3.4g fibre

tips If you have an electric pressure cooker you won't need to reduce the heat to stabilise pressure, your cooker will automatically stabilise itself. Always check with the manufacturer's instructions before using. Recipe suitable to freeze.

BEEF

BOEUF BOURGUIGNON

1½ tablespoons olive oil
400g button mushrooms
1 dried bay leaf
3 sprigs fresh parsley
1 sprig fresh thyme
1kg stewing steak, chopped
coarsely
150g streaky bacon, chopped
coarsely
1 medium brown onion (150g),
chopped finely
3 cloves garlic, crushed
160ml dry red wine
70g tomato paste
12 baby onions (300g)

1 Heat 2 teaspoons of the oil in 5.5-litre pressure cooker; cook mushrooms until browned. Remove from cooker.

2 Tie bay leaf, parsley and thyme together with kitchen string to make a bouquet garni. Heat remaining oil in cooker; cook beef, in batches, until browned. Remove from cooker.

3 Cook bacon in cooker until browned. Add chopped onion and garlic; cook, stirring, until onion softens. Return beef to cooker with wine, paste and bouquet garni; secure lid. Bring cooker to high pressure. Reduce heat to stabilise pressure; cook 35 minutes.

4 Meanwhile, peel baby onions, leaving root ends intact.

5 Release pressure using the quick release method (page 6); remove lid. Add baby onions and mushrooms; secure lid. Bring cooker to high pressure. Reduce heat to stabilise pressure; cook 10 minutes. Release pressure using the quick release method (page 6); remove lid. Discard bouquet garni; season to taste. Serve with creamy mashed potato, if liked.

prep + cook time 1 hour
serves 6
nutritional count per serving
25.9g total fat (8g saturated fat); 1935kJ (463 cal); 6.1g carbohydrate; 45.7g protein; 3.3g fibre

tips If you have an electric pressure cooker you won't need to reduce the heat to stabilise pressure, your cooker will automatically stabilise itself. Always check with the manufacturer's instructions before using. Recipe not suitable to freeze.

STEAK & KIDNEY PIE

60ml olive oil

200g chestnut mushrooms, quartered

400g ox kidney, trimmed, chopped coarsely

2 tablespoons plain flour

700g braising steak, chopped coarsely

1 medium brown onion (150g), chopped finely

1 large carrot (180g), chopped finely

1 stalk celery (150g), trimmed, chopped finely

2 sprigs fresh thyme

1 dried bay leaf

80ml water

1 sheet ready-rolled puff pastry (320g)

1 egg, beaten lightly

1 Heat 2 teaspoons of the oil in 5.5-litre pressure cooker; cook mushrooms until browned. Remove from cooker.

2 Heat 2 teaspoons of the oil in cooker; cook kidney until browned. Remove from cooker.

3 Season flour in large bowl; Add beef, toss to coat in flour. Shake off excess. Heat half the remaining oil in cooker; cook beef, in batches, until browned. Remove from cooker.

4 Heat remaining oil in cooker; cook onion, carrot and celery, stirring, until tender. Return beef to cooker with thyme, bay leaf and the water; secure lid. Bring cooker to high pressure. Reduce heat to stabilise pressure; cook 25 minutes.

5 Meanwhile, preheat oven to 210°C.

6 Release pressure using the quick release method (page 6); remove lid, discard thyme and bay leaf. Stir in mushrooms and kidney; season to taste. Spoon hot steak and kidney mixture into 1.5-litre deep ovenproof pie dish.

Place pastry over filling, trim edge; cut two small slits in centre of pastry. Brush pastry with egg. Bake pie about 25 minutes or until well browned.

prep + cook time 1 hour 10 minutes

serves 4

nutritional count per serving
35g total fat (7.2g saturated fat); 2755kJ (659 cal); 24.3g carbohydrate; 60g protein; 4.1g fibre

tips If you have an electric pressure cooker you won't need to reduce the heat to stabilise pressure, your cooker will automatically stabilise itself. Always check with the manufacturer's instructions before using. Steak and kidney filling is suitable to freeze.

CHILLI CON CARNE

400g dried red kidney beans
3 small brown onions (240g),
  peeled
1 dried bay leaf
1.5 litres water
150g streaky bacon, chopped
  finely
170g cured chorizo, chopped
  finely
400g minced beef
2 cloves garlic, crushed
2 tablespoons ground cumin
1 tablespoon ground coriander
1 teaspoon dried chilli flakes
560g bottled tomato pasta sauce
2 teaspoons dried oregano
120g soured cream
6 tablespoons fresh coriander
  leaves

1 Place beans in large bowl, cover with cold water; stand overnight. Rinse under cold water; drain.
2 Combine beans, one of the onions, bay leaf and the water in 5.5-litre pressure cooker; secure lid. Bring cooker to high pressure. Reduce heat to stabilise pressure; cook 15 minutes. Release pressure using the quick release method (page 6); remove lid. Drain beans, reserving 375ml cooking liquid; discard onion and bay leaf.
3 Finely chop remaining onions. Cook bacon and chorizo in cooker until browned. Add onion; cook, stirring, until onion softens. Add beef; cook, stirring, until browned. Add garlic and spices; cook, stirring, until fragrant. Return beans to cooker with sauce, oregano and reserved cooking liquid; season to taste. Bring cooker to high pressure. Reduce heat to stabilise pressure; cook 8 minutes. Release pressure using the quick release method (page 6); remove lid. Stand 5 minutes.
4 Serve chilli con carne with soured cream and sprinkled with coriander.

prep + cook time 40 minutes + standing time
serves 6
nutritional count per serving 34.9g total fat (15.3g saturated fat); 2913kJ (697 cal); 36.1g carbohydrate; 51.3g protein; 17.1g fibre
tips If you have an electric pressure cooker you won't need to reduce the heat to stabilise pressure, your cooker will automatically stabilise itself. Always check with the manufacturer's instructions before using. If you normally eat chilli con carne with soured cream but are trying to be good, try it with a dollop of low-fat greek-style yogurt. Recipe suitable to freeze.

BEEF TAGINE WITH SPINACH & OLIVES

1 tablespoon olive oil

1.2kg braising steak, trimmed, chopped coarsely

1 medium brown onion (150g), chopped finely

2 cloves garlic, crushed

1 teaspoon each ground allspice and dried chilli flakes

pinch saffron threads

410g canned tomatoes, crushed

125ml beef stock

300g spinach, trimmed, shredded coarsely

60g pitted green olives

2 tablespoons thinly sliced preserved lemon rind

45g roasted unsalted pistachios, coarsely chopped

1 Heat half the oil in 5.5-litre pressure cooker; cook beef, in batches, until browned. Remove from cooker.

2 Heat remaining oil in cooker; cook onion, garlic and spices, stirring, until onion softens. Return beef to cooker with undrained tomatoes and stock; secure lid. Bring cooker to high pressure. Reduce heat to stabilise pressure; cook 15 minutes.

3 Release pressure using the quick release method (page 6); remove lid. Stir in spinach, olives and preserved lemon; simmer, uncovered, until hot. Season to taste.

4 Serve tagine sprinkled with nuts and accompanied by couscous, if liked.

prep + cook time 30 minutes
serves 4
nutritional count per serving
30.5g total fat (9.8g saturated fat); 2537kJ (607 cal); 11.3g carbohydrate; 69g protein; 5.4g fibre

tips If you have an electric pressure cooker you won't need to reduce the heat to stabilise pressure, your cooker will automatically stabilise itself. Always check with the manufacturer's instructions before using. Preserved lemons, a prominent ingredient in North African cooking, are salted lemons bottled for several months; the flavour is salty, unique and perfumed. To use, discard flesh, rinse well, using rind only. Recipe not suitable to freeze. Recipe not suitable to freeze.

THAI BEEF AND COCONUT CURRY

2 x 10cm sticks fresh lemongrass (20g), chopped coarsely
4 cloves garlic, quartered
2 fresh long red chillies, chopped coarsely
4cm piece fresh ginger (20g), sliced thinly
4 kaffir lime leaves, sliced thinly
1 tablespoon tamarind paste
80ml water
1 tablespoon groundnut oil
1.2kg braising steak, trimmed, chopped coarsely
160ml coconut milk
2 medium carrots (240g), halved lengthways, sliced thinly
125g baby corn, halved lengthways
155g sugar snap peas, trimmed
1 tablespoon lime juice
2 teaspoons fish sauce
40g toasted shredded coconut
1 fresh long red chilli, sliced thinly

1 Blend or process lemongrass, garlic, chopped chilli, ginger, lime leaves, tamarind and the water until mixture forms a smooth paste.

2 Heat half the oil in 5.5-litre pressure cooker; cook beef, in batches, until browned. Remove from cooker.

3 Heat remaining oil in cooker; cook paste, stirring, about 3 minutes or until thickened slightly and fragrant. Stir in coconut milk. Return beef to cooker; secure lid. Bring cooker to high pressure. Reduce heat to stabilise pressure; cook 15 minutes.

4 Release pressure using the quick release method (page 6); remove lid. Add carrot and corn; secure lid. Bring cooker to high pressure. Reduce heat to stabilise pressure; cook 3 minutes.

5 Release pressure using the quick release method (page 6); remove lid. Add peas; simmer, uncovered, until peas are tender. Stir in juice and sauce.

6 Serve bowls of curry sprinkled with coconut and sliced chilli accompanied by steamed jasmine rice, if liked.

prep + cook time 35 minutes
serves 4
nutritional count per serving
33.5g total fat (19.6g saturated fat); 2617kJ (626 cal); 12.7g carbohydrate; 65.4g protein; 6.7g fibre

tips If you have an electric pressure cooker you won't need to reduce the heat to stabilise pressure, your cooker will automatically stabilise itself. Always check with the manufacturer's instructions before using. If you can't get hold of shredded coconut, you can use toasted dessicated coconut instead. Recipe not suitable to freeze.

CHINESE BRAISED OXTAIL

1kg beef oxtail, trimmed
125ml japanese soy sauce
60ml chinese cooking wine
55g dark brown sugar
6 cloves garlic, bruised
12cm piece fresh ginger (60g),
    peeled, sliced thickly
4 spring onions, chopped
    coarsely
2 star anise
2 cinnamon sticks
3 x 5cm strips orange rind
125ml water
2 spring onions, shredded finely

1 Cut oxtail into 4cm pieces. Combine sauce, wine, sugar, garlic, ginger, chopped onion, star anise, cinnamon, rind and the water in 5.5-litre pressure cooker; bring to the boil. Add oxtail; secure lid. Bring cooker to high pressure. Reduce heat to stabilise pressure; cook 30 minutes.

2 Release pressure using the quick release method (page 6); remove lid. Transfer oxtail to serving plate; drizzle with about 80ml of braising liquid. Sprinkle with shredded spring onions. Serve with steamed rice, if liked.

prep + cook time 40 minutes
serves 4
nutritional count per serving
67.2g total fat (25.8g saturated fat); 3595kJ (860 cal); 16.8g carbohydrate; 46g protein; 1.6g fibre

tips If you have an electric pressure cooker you won't need to reduce the heat to stabilise pressure, your cooker will automatically stabilise itself. Always check with the manufacturer's instructions before using. Recipe suitable to freeze.

VEAL IN MARSALA & MUSHROOM SAUCE

2 tablespoons plain flour
1kg diced veal
1 tablespoon olive oil
20g butter
1 medium brown onion (150g), chopped finely
2 cloves garlic, crushed
80ml marsala
125ml beef stock
375g mixed mushrooms, sliced thickly
125ml single cream
2 teaspoons finely chopped lemon thyme

1 Season flour in large bowl; add veal, toss to coat in flour. Shake off excess. Heat half the oil and half the butter in 5.5-litre pressure cooker; cook veal, in batches, until browned. Remove from cooker.
2 Heat remaining oil and butter in cooker; cook onion and garlic, stirring, until onion softens. Add marsala; simmer, uncovered, until liquid reduces by half. Return veal to cooker with stock; secure lid. Bring cooker to high pressure. Reduce heat to stabilise pressure; cook 10 minutes.
3 Release pressure using the quick release method (page 6); remove lid. Add mushrooms; secure lid. Bring cooker to high pressure. Reduce heat to stabilise pressure; cook 3 minutes.
4 Release pressure using the quick release method (page 6); remove lid. Stir in cream; simmer, uncovered, until sauce thickens slightly. Season to taste. Serve veal sprinkled with thyme and accompanied by pasta or creamy mashed potato, if liked.

prep + cook time 25 minutes
serves 4
nutritional count per serving
27.1g total fat (13.8g saturated fat); 2433kJ (582 cal); 11.2g carbohydrate; 66.1g protein; 3.3g fibre

tips If you have an electric pressure cooker you won't need to reduce the heat to stabilise pressure, your cooker will automatically stabilise itself. Always check with the manufacturer's instructions before using. Ask the butcher for any stewing veal, such as shoulder. Recipe not suitable to freeze.

BEEF POT ROAST

1 tablespoon olive oil
1.2kg piece beef topside
8 baby brown onions (200g)
315g baby carrots, trimmed
2 medium parsnips (500g),
  chopped coarsely
500g baby new potatoes
40g butter
2 tablespoons plain flour
375ml beef stock
80ml dry red wine
1 tablespoon tomato paste
1 tablespoon worcestershire
  sauce

1 Heat oil in 5.5-litre pressure cooker; cook beef until browned all over. Remove from cooker.
2 Peel onions, leaving root ends intact. Cook onions, carrots, parsnip and potatoes in cooker, stirring, until browned lightly. Remove vegetables from cooker.
3 Melt butter in cooker; add flour, cook, stirring, until browned lightly. Gradually stir in stock and wine; cook, stirring, until sauce boils and thickens. Stir in paste and sauce.
4 Return beef to cooker; secure lid. Bring cooker to high pressure. Reduce heat to stabilise pressure; cook 20 minutes.
5 Release pressure using the quick release method (page 6); remove lid. Return vegetables to cooker; secure lid. Bring cooker to high pressure. Reduce heat to stabilise pressure; cook 7 minutes.
6 Release pressure using the quick release method (page 6); remove lid. Remove beef and vegetables, cover; stand 10 minutes then slice beef thinly. Strain sauce into medium heatproof jug; season to taste.

7 Serve beef with vegetables and sauce, accompanied by steamed seasonal vegetables, if liked.

prep + cook time 45 minutes
serves 4
nutritional count per serving
23.1g total fat (10g saturated fat); 2901kJ (694 cal); 40.2g carbohydrate; 73g protein; 8.7g fibre
tips If you have an electric pressure cooker you won't need to reduce the heat to stabilise pressure, your cooker will automatically stabilise itself. Always check with the manufacturer's instructions before using. Recipe not suitable to freeze.

BEEF, BLACK BEAN & CORN STEW

200g dried black beans
1 tablespoon olive oil
1kg braising steak, trimmed, chopped coarsely
1 large brown onion (200g), chopped finely
2 cloves garlic, crushed
2 teaspoons ground cumin
1 teaspoon dried chilli flakes
410g canned tomatoes, crushed
375ml beef stock
1 medium red pepper (200g), sliced thinly
2 trimmed corn cobs (500g), kernels removed
2 medium tomatoes (300g), sliced thinly
6 tablespoons coarsely chopped fresh coriander
1 medium lime, cut into wedges

1 Place beans in medium bowl, cover with cold water; stand overnight. Rinse under cold water; drain.

2 Heat half the oil in 5.5-litre pressure cooker; cook beef, in batches, until browned. Remove from cooker.

3 Heat remaining oil in cooker; cook onion and garlic, stirring, until onion softens. Add spices; cook, stirring, until fragrant. Return beef to cooker with undrained tomatoes, stock and beans; secure lid. Bring cooker to high pressure. Reduce heat to stabilise pressure; cook 25 minutes.

4 Release pressure using the quick release method (page 6); remove lid. Add pepper and corn; secure lid. Bring cooker to high pressure. Reduce heat to stabilise pressure; cook 2 minutes.

5 Release pressure using the quick release method (page 6); remove lid. Stir in tomato and coriander; season to taste. Serve stew with lime wedges.

prep + cook time 45 minutes
serves 6
nutritional count per serving 18.4g total fat (4.7g saturated fat); 1919kJ (459 cal); 18.4g carbohydrate; 49.2g protein; 11.7g fibre
tips If you have an electric pressure cooker you won't need to reduce the heat to stabilise pressure, your cooker will automatically stabilise itself. Always check with the manufacturer's instructions before using. Recipe suitable to freeze.

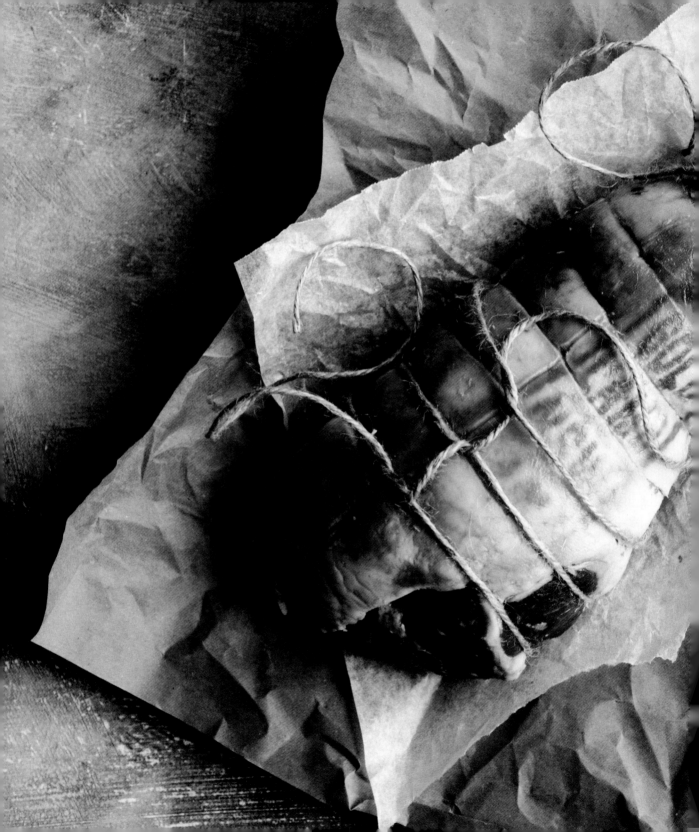

LAMB

NAVARIN OF LAMB

1 tablespoon olive oil

4 lamb neck chops (680g), trimmed

1 large brown onion (200g), chopped finely

2 cloves garlic, crushed

410g canned chopped tomatoes

125ml water

8 baby brown onions (200g)

500g baby new potatoes, halved

400g baby carrots, trimmed, peeled

120g frozen peas

2 tablespoons coarsely chopped fresh flat-leaf parsley

1 Heat oil in 5.5-litre pressure cooker; cook lamb, in batches, until browned. Remove from cooker.

2 Cook chopped onion and garlic in cooker, stirring, until onion softens. Return lamb to cooker with undrained tomatoes and the water; secure lid. Bring cooker to high pressure. Reduce heat to stabilise pressure; cook 15 minutes.

3 Meanwhile, peel baby onions, leaving root ends intact.

4 Release cooker pressure using the quick release method (page 6); remove lid. Stir in potato and onions, top with carrots; secure lid. Bring cooker to high pressure. Reduce heat to stabilise pressure; cook 5 minutes.

5 Release pressure using the quick release method (page 6); remove lid. Add peas; simmer, uncovered, until peas are tender and season to taste. Serve sprinkled with parsley.

prep + cook time 40 minutes
serves 4
nutritional count per serving
21.9g total fat (8.3g saturated fat); 1994kJ (477 cal); 31.2g carbohydrate; 34g protein; 9.6g fibre

tips If you have an electric pressure cooker you won't need to reduce the heat to stabilise pressure, your cooker will automatically stabilise itself. Always check with the manufacturer's instructions before using. Recipe not suitable to freeze.

GREEK-STYLE LAMB CASSEROLE

2 tablespoons plain flour

1kg boned lamb shoulder, trimmed, chopped coarsely

2 tablespoons olive oil

1 medium brown onion (150g), sliced thinly

3 cloves garlic, crushed

410g canned tomatoes, crushed

80ml dry white wine

80ml chicken stock

4 tablespoons coarsely chopped fresh oregano

60g pitted black olives

1 teaspoon finely grated lemon rind

3 tablespoons fresh oregano leaves

1 medium lemon, cut into wedges

1 Season flour in large bowl; add lamb, toss to coat in flour. Shake off excess. Heat half the oil in 5.5-litre pressure cooker; cook lamb, in batches, until browned. Remove from cooker.

2 Heat remaining oil in cooker; cook onion and garlic, stirring, until onion softens. Return lamb to cooker with undrained tomatoes, wine, stock and half the chopped oregano; secure lid. Bring cooker to high pressure. Reduce heat to stabilise pressure; cook 25 minutes.

3 Release pressure using the quick release method (page 6); remove lid. Stir in remaining chopped oregano, olives and rind; season to taste.

4 Serve casserole sprinkled with oregano leaves and lemon wedges and accompanied by creamy mashed potato or roast potatoes, if liked.

prep + cook time 35 minutes
serves 4
nutritional count per serving
32g total fat (11.6g saturated fat); 2337kJ (559 cal); 13.1g carbohydrate; 50.7g protein; 2.5g fibre

tips If you have an electric pressure cooker you won't need to reduce the heat to stabilise pressure, your cooker will automatically stabilise itself. Always check with the manufacturer's instructions before using. Recipe suitable to freeze.

WHITE WINE & LAMB ONE POT

2 tablespoons olive oil

800g boned lamb leg, chopped coarsely

1 large brown onion (200g), chopped finely

250ml dry white wine

600g waxy potatoes, peeled, chopped coarsely

240g frozen peas

3 eggs

40g finely grated parmesan cheese, plus extra to serve

4 tablespoons coarsely chopped fresh flat-leaf parsley

1 Heat oil in 5.5-litre pressure cooker; cook lamb, in batches, until browned. Remove from cooker.

2 Cook onion in cooker, stirring, until soft. Return lamb to cooker with wine; secure lid. Bring cooker to high pressure. Reduce heat to stabilise pressure; cook 20 minutes.

3 Release pressure using the quick release method (page 6); remove lid. Add potato; secure lid. Bring cooker to high pressure. Reduce heat to stabilise pressure; cook 5 minutes.

4 Release pressure using the quick release method (page 6); remove lid. Add peas; simmer, uncovered, until peas are tender. Remove from heat.

5 Whisk eggs and cheese in medium bowl; stir into hot lamb mixture until sauce thickens. Season to taste. Serve sprinkled with parsley and extra grated parmesan cheese.

prep + cook time 45 minutes
serves 4
nutritional count per serving
27.4g total fat (9.4g saturated fat); 2571kJ (615 cal); 19.5g carbohydrate; 59.6g protein; 5.6g fibre

tips If you have an electric pressure cooker you won't need to reduce the heat to stabilise pressure, your cooker will automatically stabilise itself. Always check with the manufacturer's instructions before using. Thickening a sauce with eggs at the end of cooking is done in many European countries such as Italy and Greece. Recipe not suitable to freeze.

LEMON & GINGER LAMB SHANKS WITH BROAD BEANS

1 tablespoon olive oil
4 french-trimmed lamb shanks
    (1kg)
1 large brown onion (200g),
    chopped finely
3 cloves garlic, crushed
2 tablespoons thinly sliced
    preserved lemon rind
5cm piece fresh ginger (25g),
    grated
1 cinnamon stick
60ml lemon juice
125ml water
300g frozen broad beans
600g waxy potatoes, halved
20g butter
good handful finely chopped
    fresh coriander
6 tablespoons finely chopped
    fresh flat-leaf parsley

1 Heat half the oil in 5.5-litre pressure cooker; cook lamb, in batches, until browned. Remove from cooker.
2 Heat remaining oil in cooker; cook onion and garlic, stirring, until onion softens. Add preserved lemon, ginger and cinnamon; cook, stirring, until fragrant. Return lamb to cooker with juice and the water; secure lid. Bring cooker to high pressure. Reduce heat to stabilise pressure; cook 25 minutes.
3 Meanwhile, cook beans in large saucepan of boiling water about 2 minutes or until tender; drain. Rinse under cold water; drain. Peel away grey skins.
4 Release pressure using the quick release method (page 6); remove lid. Add potato; secure lid. Bring cooker to high pressure. Reduce heat to stabilise pressure; cook 10 minutes.
5 Meanwhile, melt butter in medium frying pan; cook herbs, stirring, until bright green.
6 Release cooker pressure using the quick release method (page 6); remove lid. Stir in beans and herbs; simmer, uncovered until hot. Season to taste.

prep + cook time 50 minutes
serves 4
nutritional count per serving
21.5g total fat (9g saturated fat); 1952kJ (467 cal); 26.5g carbohydrate; 36.4g protein; 11.5g fibre

tips If you have an electric pressure cooker you won't need to reduce the heat to stabilise pressure, your cooker will automatically stabilise itself. Always check with the manufacturer's instructions before using. To use preserved lemon, discard flesh, rinse well, using rind only. Recipe not suitable to freeze.

CURRIED LAMB IN YOGURT SAUCE

1 tablespoon vegetable oil

1kg boned lamb shoulder, trimmed, chopped coarsely

2 medium brown onions (300g), sliced thinly

3 cloves garlic, crushed

2.5cm piece fresh ginger (15g), grated

2 teaspoons ground cumin

1 teaspoon ground cinnamon

½ teaspoon each ground cardamom, fennel and turmeric

560g natural yogurt

1 tablespoon cornflour

2 tablespoons water

6 tablespoons fresh coriander leaves

1 Heat half the oil in 5.5-litre pressure cooker; cook lamb, in batches, until browned. Remove from cooker.

2 Heat remaining oil in cooker; cook onion, garlic and ginger, stirring, until onion softens. Add spices; cook, stirring, until fragrant. Return lamb to cooker with yogurt; secure lid. Bring cooker to high pressure. Reduce heat to stabilise pressure; cook 25 minutes.

3 Release pressure using the quick release method (page 6); remove lid. Stir in blended cornflour and the water; stir until sauce boils and thickens slightly. Season to taste.

4 Serve curry sprinkled with coriander, accompanied by steamed basmati rice and warm naan bread, if liked.

prep + cook time 35 minutes
serves 4
nutritional count per serving
31.8g total fat (13.9g saturated fat); 2370kJ (567 cal); 13.4g carbohydrate; 56.2g protein; 1.8g fibre

tips If you have an electric pressure cooker you won't need to reduce the heat to stabilise pressure, your cooker will automatically stabilise itself. Always check with the manufacturer's instructions before using. Recipe not suitable to freeze.

BRAISED LAMB SHOULDER WITH BORLOTTI BEANS

300g dried borlotti beans
700g boned lamb shoulder
2 tablespoons olive oil
2 medium brown onions (300g), chopped finely
2 stalks celery (300g), trimmed, chopped finely
1 large carrot (180g), chopped finely
2 cloves garlic, crushed
410g canned chopped tomatoes
2 sprigs fresh rosemary
500ml water

1 Place beans in large bowl, cover with cold water; stand overnight. Rinse under cold water; drain.

2 Roll lamb tightly; tie with kitchen string, at 2cm intervals, to secure. Season lamb. Heat half the oil in 5.5-litre pressure cooker; cook lamb until browned all over. Remove from cooker.

3 Add remaining oil to cooker; cook onion, celery and carrot, stirring, until vegetables soften. Add garlic; cook, stirring, until fragrant. Stir in beans, undrained tomatoes, rosemary and the water. Return lamb to cooker; secure lid. Bring cooker to high pressure. Reduce heat to stabilise pressure; cook 25 minutes.

4 Release pressure using the quick release method (page 6); remove lid. Remove lamb, cover loosely; stand 5 minutes. Secure lid of cooker; bring cooker to high pressure. Reduce heat to stabilise pressure; cook 5 minutes. Release pressure using the quick release method (page 6); remove lid. Discard rosemary; season to taste. Serve sliced lamb with bean mixture and crusty bread, if liked.

prep + cook time 50 minutes + standing time
serves 4
nutritional count per serving 26.4g total fat (8.6g saturated fat); 2667kJ (638 cal); 36.7g carbohydrate; 53.2g protein; 20.6g fibre
tips If you have an electric pressure cooker you won't need to reduce the heat to stabilise pressure, your cooker will automatically stabilise itself. Always check with the manufacturer's instructions before using. Recipe not suitable to freeze.

HOT-PEPPERED LAMB CURRY

2 fresh long green chillies
2 tablespoons ghee or butter
600g boned lamb leg, chopped
  coarsely
2 large brown onions (400g),
  sliced thinly
3 cloves garlic, crushed
4cm piece fresh ginger (20g),
  grated
3 cloves
4 green cardamom pods, bruised
2 cinnamon sticks
2 teaspoons coarsely ground
  black pepper
2 medium tomatoes (300g),
  chopped finely
70g natural yogurt
125ml water
60ml lemon juice
4 tablespoons finely chopped
  fresh coriander

1 Finely chop 1 of the chillies; finely shred remaining chilli.
2 Heat half the ghee or butter in 5.5-litre pressure cooker; cook lamb, in batches, until browned. Remove from cooker.
3 Heat remaining ghee or butter in same cooker; cook onion, stirring, about 5 minutes or until browned lightly. Add garlic and ginger; cook, stirring, until fragrant. Return lamb to cooker with spices, tomato, chopped chilli, yogurt and the water; secure lid. Bring cooker to high pressure. Reduce heat to stabilise pressure; cook 25 minutes.
4 Release pressure using the quick release method (page 6); remove lid. Stir in juice; season to taste. Serve sprinkled with coriander and shredded chilli and accompanied by steamed white long-grain rice, if liked.

prep + cook time 1 hour
serves 4
nutritional count per serving
17.7g total fat (9.7g saturated fat); 1442kJ (345 cal); 8.6g carbohydrate; 36.5g protein; 3g fibre

tips If you have an electric pressure cooker you won't need to reduce the heat to stabilise pressure, your cooker will automatically stabilise itself. Always check with the manufacturer's instructions before using. This is a hot curry. If you prefer a milder version, reduce the amount of pepper and chilli. You can also serve it with an extra dollop of yogurt if you like. Recipe suitable to freeze.

PERSIAN LAMB WITH ROASTED RHUBARB

60g butter
700g boned lamb shoulder,
    trimmed, chopped coarsely
1 large brown onion (200g),
    chopped finely
3 teaspoons ground coriander
125ml water
6 tablespoons finely chopped
    fresh mint
3 tablespoons finely chopped
    fresh flat-leaf parsley

roasted rhubarb
5 trimmed large stems rhubarb
    (300g), chopped coarsely
75g caster sugar
25g unsalted butter, chopped
    finely

1 Melt 20g of the butter in 5.5-litre pressure cooker; cook lamb, in batches, until browned. Remove from cooker.
2 Melt half the remaining butter in cooker; cook onion, stirring, until soft. Add coriander; cook, stirring, until fragrant. Return lamb to cooker with the water; secure lid. Bring cooker to high pressure. Reduce heat to stabilise pressure; cook 25 minutes.
3 Meanwhile, make roasted rhubarb.
4 Melt remaining butter in medium frying pan; cook herbs, stirring, until bright green.
5 Release cooker pressure using quick release method (page 6); remove lid. Stir in herbs, season to taste. Serve lamb topped with rhubarb and accompanied by couscous, if liked.

roasted rhubarb Preheat oven to 200°C. Arrange rhubarb, in single layer, in large baking dish. Sprinkle with sugar; dot with butter. Bake about 15 minutes or until rhubarb is tender but still holds its shape.

prep + cook time 40 minutes
serves 4
nutritional count per serving
33.3g total fat (18.7g saturated fat); 2261kJ (541 cal); 23.2g carbohydrate; 36g protein; 3.7g fibre
tips If you have an electric pressure cooker you won't need to reduce the heat to stabilise pressure, your cooker will automatically stabilise itself. Always check with the manufacturer's instructions before using. Frying the herbs in butter, rather than adding them directly to the sauce, gives them extra flavour and keeps them bright green. Recipe not suitable to freeze.

COUNTRY LAMB & BARLEY STEW

2 tablespoons plain flour
1kg boned lamb leg, chopped
    coarsely
1 tablespoon olive oil
8 baby brown onions (200g)
500ml chicken stock
130g pearl barley
3 sprigs fresh thyme, plus extra
    to serve
2 celery stalks (300g), trimmed,
    chopped coarsely
2 medium carrots (240g),
    chopped coarsely
400g baby new potatoes,
    quartered

1 Season flour in large bowl; add lamb, toss to coat in flour. Shake off excess. Heat half the oil in 5.5-litre pressure cooker; cook lamb, in batches, until browned. Remove from cooker.

2 Meanwhile, peel onions, leaving root ends intact; halve.

3 Heat remaining oil in cooker; cook onion, stirring, until browned lightly. Remove from cooker. Return lamb to cooker with stock, barley and thyme; secure lid. Bring cooker to high pressure. Reduce heat to stabilise pressure; cook 20 minutes.

4 Release pressure using the quick release method (page 6); remove lid. Add onion, celery, carrot and potato; secure lid. Bring cooker to high pressure. Reduce heat to stabilise pressure; cook 7 minutes.

5 Release pressure using the quick release method (page 6); remove lid. Season stew to taste; serve sprinkled with thyme leaves and accompanied by crusty bread, if liked.

prep + cook time 40 minutes
serves 6
nutritional count per serving
13.1g total fat (4.7g saturated fat); 1747kJ (418 cal); 29.2g carbohydrate; 42.5g protein; 6g fibre

tips If you have an electric pressure cooker you won't need to reduce the heat to stabilise pressure, your cooker will automatically stabilise itself. Always check with the manufacturer's instructions before using. Recipe suitable to freeze.

DESSERTS

FIG BREAD & BUTTER PUDDING

4 slices white crusty bread (150g)
20g butter, softened
80g fig jam
55g sultanas
¼ teaspoon ground nutmeg

custard
310ml milk
250ml double cream
55g caster sugar
1 teaspoon vanilla extract
3 eggs

1 Grease 1.25-litre, 16-cm round ovenproof dish.

2 Make custard.

3 Spread each slice of bread with butter and jam; cut into four triangles. Layer bread, overlapping, in dish; sprinkle with sultanas. Pour half the custard over bread; stand 2 minutes. Pour remaining custard into dish. Sprinkle with nutmeg; cover tightly with foil.

4 Place steamer basket in 5.5-litre pressure cooker; add 375ml water. Place dish on a tea towel; use tea towel to lower dish into basket in cooker. Fold tea towel overhang over top of dish; secure lid of cooker. Bring cooker to low pressure. Reduce heat to stabilise pressure; cook 15 minutes.

5 Release pressure using the quick release method (page 6); remove lid. Remove dish from cooker; stand 5 minutes before serving.

custard Combine milk, cream, sugar and extract in medium saucepan; bring to the boil. Whisk eggs in large bowl; gradually whisk hot milk mixture into egg mixture.

prep + cook time 35 minutes
serves 6
nutritional count per serving
26.1g total fat (15.9g saturated fat); 1789kJ (428 cal); 39.8g carbohydrate; 8.3g protein; 1.3g fibre

tips If you have an electric pressure cooker you won't need to reduce the heat to stabilise pressure, your cooker will automatically stabilise itself. Always check with the manufacturer's instructions before using. Recipe not suitable to freeze.

CARAMEL BANANA STEAMED PUDDING

90g butter, softened
110g light brown sugar
1 egg yolk
1 egg
200g mashed banana
185g self-raising flour
1 teaspoon ground cinnamon
80ml milk

caramel sauce
110g light brown sugar
125ml double cream
55g butter, chopped

1 Grease 1.25-litre, 16-cm round ovenproof dish.
2 Make caramel sauce. Pour half the sauce into dish.
3 Beat butter, sugar and yolk in small bowl with electric mixer until light and fluffy. Beat in egg; transfer to large bowl. Stir in banana, then sifted dry ingredients and milk, in two batches. Spoon mixture into dish; cover tightly with foil.
4 Place steamer basket in 5.5-litre pressure cooker; add 500ml water. Place dish on a tea towel; use tea towel to lower dish into basket in cooker. Fold tea towel overhang over top of dish; secure lid of cooker. Bring cooker to high pressure. Reduce heat to stabilise pressure; cook 32 minutes.
5 Release pressure using the quick release method (page 6); remove lid. Remove dish from cooker; serve pudding drizzled with remaining caramel sauce.

caramel sauce Combine ingredients in small saucepan; stir over heat, without boiling, until sugar dissolves. Reduce heat; simmer, stirring, about 3 minutes or until thickened slightly.

prep + cook time 50 minutes
serves 4
nutritional count per serving
47.3g total fat (29.9g saturated fat); 3549kJ (849 cal); 95.6g carbohydrate; 9.2g protein; 2.7g fibre
tips If you have an electric pressure cooker you won't need to reduce the heat to stabilise pressure, your cooker will automatically stabilise itself. Always check with the manufacturer's instructions before using. You will need 2 small over-ripe bananas (260g). Recipe not suitable to freeze.

ORANGE CREME CARAMEL

220g caster sugar
125ml water
300ml double cream
310ml milk
2 teaspoons finely grated orange
  rind
3 eggs
2 egg yolks
1 teaspoon vanilla extract
55g caster sugar, extra

1 Combine sugar and the water in medium heavy-based frying pan; stir over heat, without boiling, until sugar dissolves. Bring to the boil; boil, uncovered, without stirring, until mixture is a deep caramel colour. Remove from heat; allow bubbles to subside. Pour toffee into 1.25-litre, 16-cm round ovenproof dish.
2 Combine cream, milk and rind in medium saucepan; bring to the boil.
3 Meanwhile, whisk eggs, yolks, extract and extra sugar in large bowl. Whisk hot milk mixture into egg mixture. Strain mixture into dish; cover tightly with foil.
4 Place steamer basket in 5.5-litre pressure cooker; add 375ml water. Place dish on a tea towel; use tea towel to lower dish into basket in cooker. Fold tea towel overhang over top of dish; secure lid of cooker. Bring cooker to low pressure. Reduce heat to stabilise pressure; cook 30 minutes.
5 Release pressure using the quick release method (page 6); remove lid. Remove dish from cooker; cool 15 minutes. Refrigerate overnight.
6 Gently ease crème caramel from side of dish; invert onto deep-sided serving plate. Serve with whipped or double cream and orange segments, if liked.

prep + cook time 45 minutes + cooling & refrigeration time
serves 4
nutritional count per serving
38.6g total fat (23g saturated fat); 2888kJ (691 cal); 75.2g carbohydrate; 10.8g protein; 0g fibre
tips If you have an electric pressure cooker you won't need to reduce the heat to stabilise pressure, your cooker will automatically stabilise itself. Always check with the manufacturer's instructions before using. Recipe not suitable to freeze.

LEMON DELICIOUS

75g butter, melted
2 teaspoons finely grated lemon
  rind
220g caster sugar
2 eggs, separated
75g self-raising flour
60ml lemon juice
180ml milk
2 teaspoons icing sugar

1 Grease 1.25-litre, 16-cm round ovenproof dish.
2 Combine butter, rind, sugar and yolks in medium bowl. Whisk in sifted flour then juice. Gradually whisk in milk; mixture should be smooth and runny.
3 Beat egg whites in small bowl with electric mixer until soft peaks form; fold into lemon mixture in two batches.
4 Spoon lemon mixture into dish; cover tightly with foil. Place steamer basket in 5.5-litre pressure cooker; add 375ml water. Place dish on a tea towel; use tea towel to lower dish into basket in cooker. Fold tea towel overhang over top of dish; secure lid of cooker. Bring cooker to high pressure. Reduce heat to stabilise pressure; cook 27 minutes.
5 Release pressure using the quick release method (page 6); remove lid. Remove dish from cooker, dust lemon delicious with sifted icing sugar; serve immediately.

prep + cook time 45 minutes
serves 4
nutritional count per serving
20g total fat (12.1g saturated fat); 2069kJ (495 cal); 71.1g carbohydrate; 6.9g protein; 0.8g fibre
tips If you have an electric pressure cooker you won't need to reduce the heat to stabilise pressure, your cooker will automatically stabilise itself. Always check with the manufacturer's instructions before using. Recipe not suitable to freeze.

BUTTERSCOTCH APPLES

110g light brown sugar
125ml apple juice
4 large green apples (800g),
    peeled, quartered, cored
125ml double cream
45g butter

1 Combine sugar and juice in 5.5-litre pressure cooker. Add apples; turn to coat in mixture. Secure lid; bring cooker to low pressure. Reduce heat to stabilise pressure; cook 6 minutes.
2 Release pressure using the quick release method (page 6); remove lid. Remove apples from cooker; transfer to serving plates.
3 Add cream and butter to cooker; simmer, stirring occasionally, about 5 minutes or until sauce is thickened slightly. Serve apples drizzled with sauce and accompanied by single cream, if liked.

prep + cook time 20 minutes
serves 4
nutritional count per serving
22.9g total fat (15g saturated fat); 1693kJ (405 cal); 47.4g carbohydrate; 1.2g protein; 2.8g fibre
tips If you have an electric pressure cooker you won't need to reduce the heat to stabilise pressure, your cooker will automatically stabilise itself. Always check with the manufacturer's instructions before using. Recipe not suitable to freeze.

QUINCES IN ORANGE-VANILLA SYRUP

4 medium quinces (1.4kg)
500ml water
440g caster sugar
2 teaspoons vanilla extract
4 x 5cm strips orange rind
80ml orange juice
80ml orange-flavoured liqueur

1 Peel, quarter and core quinces. Cut each quarter into two wedges.
2 Combine remaining ingredients in 5.5-litre pressure cooker; cook, stirring, until sugar dissolves. Add quince; turn to coat in orange mixture. Secure lid; bring cooker to low pressure. Reduce heat to stabilise pressure; cook 40 minutes.
3 Release pressure using the quick release method (page 6); remove lid. Turn quinces in syrup; cool in cooker. Serve quinces drizzled with syrup and accompanied by whipped cream, ice-cream or custard, if liked.

prep + cook time 1 hour + cooling time
serves 6
nutritional count per serving 0.4g total fat (0g saturated fat); 1935kJ (463 cal); 98.5g carbohydrate; 0.9g protein; 12.1g fibre
tips If you have an electric pressure cooker you won't need to reduce the heat to stabilise pressure, your cooker will automatically stabilise itself. Always check with the manufacturer's instructions before using. Recipe not suitable to freeze.

GOLDEN SYRUP DUMPLINGS

185g self-raising flour
30g butter
115g golden syrup
80ml milk

golden syrup sauce
30g butter
165g light brown sugar
175g golden syrup
410ml water

1 Sift flour into medium bowl; rub in butter. Stir in golden syrup and milk in two batches.
2 Make golden syrup sauce.
3 Drop rounded tablespoonfuls of mixture into sauce; secure lid of cooker. Bring cooker to high pressure. Reduce heat to stabilise pressure; cook 8 minutes.
4 Release pressure using the quick release method (page 6); remove lid. Serve dumplings with sauce and single cream or ice-cream, if liked.

golden syrup sauce Combine ingredients in 5.5-litre pressure cooker; simmer, stirring, until sugar dissolves and sauce is hot.

prep + cook time 35 minutes
serves 4
nutritional count per serving
13.6g total fat (8.7g saturated fat); 2784kJ (666 cal); 127.9g carbohydrate; 5.6g protein; 1.8g fibre
tips If you have an electric pressure cooker you won't need to reduce the heat to stabilise pressure, your cooker will automatically stabilise itself. Always check with the manufacturer's instructions before using. Recipe not suitable to freeze.

GLOSSARY

allspice also known as pimento or Jamaican pepper; available whole or ground.

anchovies small, silvery, oily fish native to the Mediterranean; usually sold preserved in salt and packed in oil or brine. Anchovies have a strong flavour and should be used sparingly.

beans

black also known as turtle beans or black kidney beans, these earthy-flavoured dried beans are different from Chinese black beans (which are fermented soy beans). Mostly used in Mexico, South- and Central-America and the Caribbean, especially in soups and stews.

borlotti also known as roman beans, they can be eaten fresh or dried. They are a pale pink or beige colour with darker red spots.

red kidney pink to maroon beans with a floury texture and fairly sweet flavour; sold dried or tinned.

capers grey-green buds of a warm climate (usually Mediterranean) shrub, sold either dried and salted or pickled in brine. Rinse well before using.

chinese cooking wine also called shao hsing or chinese rice wine; made from fermented rice, wheat, sugar and salt with a 13.5 per cent alcohol content. Used for marinades and as a sauce ingredient, it can be purchased from most Asian food stores and some supermarkets; if you can't find it, replace with mirin or sherry.

chorizo sausage of Spanish origin; made of coarsely ground pork and highly seasoned with garlic and chillies.

coconut

cream available in tins and cartons; as a rule, the proportions are two parts coconut to one part water.

milk unsweetened coconut milk available in cans

shredded thin strips of dried coconut.

fennel bulb vegetable, also known as finocchio or anise. Also the name given to dried seeds which have a liquorice flavour.

fish sauce also called nam pla or nuoc nam; made from pulverised salted fermented fish, mostly anchovies. Has a pungent smell and strong taste; use sparingly.

five-spice powder a fragrant mixture of ground cinnamon, cloves, star anise, sichuan pepper and fennel seeds.

garam masala a blend of spices based on varying proportions of cardamom, cinnamon, cloves, coriander, fennel and cumin, roasted and ground together. Black pepper and chilli can be added for a hotter version.

ghee clarified butter; with the milk solids removed, this fat can be heated to a very high temperature without burning.

jalapeño chillies fairly hot green chillies. Available in brine bottled or fresh from supermarkets.

japanese soy sauce made from fermented soy beans, Japanese soy sauce tends to be clearer and thinner than Chinese varieties with a sweeter, milder flavour. The recipe includes roasted wheat in and is brewed for many months.

kaffir lime leaves aromatic leaves used fresh or dried in Asian dishes.

kecap manis also called ketjap manis; an Indonesian sweet, thick soy sauce which has sugar and spices added.

lemongrass a tall, clumping, lemon-smelling and tasting, sharp edged grass; use only the white lower part of each stem.

lentils (red, brown, yellow) dried pulses often identified by and named after their colour.

maple syrup distilled from the sap of maple trees found only in Canada and parts of North America. Maple-flavoured syrup is not an adequate substitute for the real thing.

marsala a fortified Italian wine recognisable by its intense amber colour and complex aroma.

olives

black have a richer and more mellow flavour than the green ones and are softer in texture.

green harvested before fully ripened and denser and more bitter than their black relatives.

kalamata black olive from Kalamata in Greece.

palm sugar also called nam tan pip, jaggery, jawa or gula melaka; made from the sap of the sugar palm tree. Light brown to black in colour; usually sold in rock-hard cakes or grated. Available from some supermarkets and Asian food stores. If unavailable, use brown sugar.

pancetta an Italian salt-cured pork roll, usually cut from the belly; used, chopped, in cooked dishes to add flavours. Bacon can be substituted.

paprika ground dried red pepper; available sweet, smoked or hot.

parmesan a sharp-tasting, dry, hard cheese, made from skimmed or semi-skimmed milk and aged for at least a year.

pearl barley the husk is removed, then hulled and polished so that the 'pearl' of the original grain remains, much the same as white rice.

pistachios pale green, delicately flavoured nut inside hard off-white shells. To peel, soak shelled nuts in boiling water about 5 minutes; drain, then pat dry.

preserved lemon a North African specialty, the citrus is preserved, usually whole, in a mixture of salt and lemon juice or oil. To use, remove and discard pulp, squeeze juice from rind, then rinse rind well before slicing thinly. Available from most supermarkets and delicatessens.

quince A yellow-skinned fruit with hard texture and astringent, tart taste. Once cooked, quinces turn a deep-pink-ruby-salmon colour.

rice

arborio small, round-grain rice; especially suitable for risottos.

jasmine Sometimes sold as Thai fragrant rice, Jasmine rice is so-named due to its sweet aroma. Available from supermarkets and Asian food stores.

long-grain elongated grain, remains separate when cooked; most popular steaming rice in Asia.

saffron One of the most expensive spices in the world, true saffron comes only from the saffron crocus, that can produce several flowers a year.

sauerkraut fermented, salted cabbage from the German kitchen.

shallots also called french shallots, golden shallots or eschalots; small, elongated, brown-skinned members of the onion family. Grows in tight clusters similar to garlic.

soy sauce made from fermented soy beans; several variations are available.

star anise a dried star-shaped pod, the seeds of which taste of aniseed.

tamarind the tamarind tree produces clusters of hairy brown pods, each of which is filled with seeds and a viscous pulp, that are dried and pressed into blocks. Releases a sweet-sour, slightly astringent taste. Tamarind paste is available from most supermarkets.

thai basil different from sweet basil in both look and taste, with smaller leaves and purplish stems. It has a slight aniseed taste.

vinegar

balsamic authentic only from the province of Modena, Italy; made from a regional wine of white trebbiano grapes specially processed then aged in antique wooden casks to give the exquisite pungent flavour.

red wine based on fermented red wine.

white wine based on fermented white wine.

worcestershire sauce a thin, dark-brown, spicy sauce used as seasoning for meat and gravies, and as a condiment.

INDEX

CONVERSION CHARTS

measures

One metric tablespoon holds 20ml; one metric teaspoon holds 5ml.

All cup and spoon measurements are level. The most accurate way of measuring dry ingredients is to weigh them. When measuring liquids, use a clear glass or plastic jug with metric markings.

We use large eggs with an average weight of 60g.

dry measures

METRIC	IMPERIAL
15g	½oz
30g	1oz
60g	2oz
90g	3oz
125g	4oz (¼lb)
155g	5oz
185g	6oz
220g	7oz
250g	8oz (½lb)
280g	9oz
315g	10oz
345g	11oz
375g	12oz (¾lb)
410g	13oz
440g	14oz
470g	15oz
500g	16oz (1lb)
750g	24oz (1½lb)
1kg	32oz (2lb)

liquid measures

METRIC	IMPERIAL
30ml	1 fluid oz
60ml	2 fluid oz
100ml	3 fluid oz
125ml	4 fluid oz
150ml	5 fluid oz
190ml	6 fluid oz
250ml	8 fluid oz
300ml	10 fluid oz
500ml	16 fluid oz
600ml	20 fluid oz
1000ml (1 litre)	32 fluid oz

length measures

METRIC	IMPERIAL
3mm	⅛in
6mm	¼in
1cm	½in
2cm	¾in
2.5cm	1in
5cm	2in
6cm	2½in
8cm	3in
10cm	4in
13cm	5in
15cm	6in
18cm	7in
20cm	8in
23cm	9in
25cm	10in
28cm	11in
30cm	12in (1ft)

oven temperatures

These are fan-assisted temperatures. If you have a conventional oven (ie. not fan-assisted), increase temperatures by 10–20°.

	°C (CELSIUS)	°F (FAHRENHEIT)	GAS MARK
Very low	100	210	½
Low	130	260	1–2
Moderately low	140	280	3
Moderate	160	325	4–5
Moderately hot	180	350	6
Hot	200	400	7–8
Very hot	220	425	9